TIRANA TRAVEL GUIDE 2023/2024

A Pocket size Enticing Guide to Exploring the beauty of Tirana like a Local

Copyright © [2023] [Peter .M. Bece]

All rights reserved. No part of this book may be reproduced or utilized in any form or by any means, electronic or mechanical, including photocopying, recording, or by any information storage and retrieval system, without permission in writing from the author/publisher.

Valias
Kamëz
SH53
Brrar
Laknas
Kodër e Kuqe
Paskuqan
SH2
SH47
Kashar
Shkozë
Tirana
Çollak
SH56
Farkë e Madhe
Vaqarr
E852
Lundër 1
Dajas
Helmes
SH3
SH3
Bërzhitë

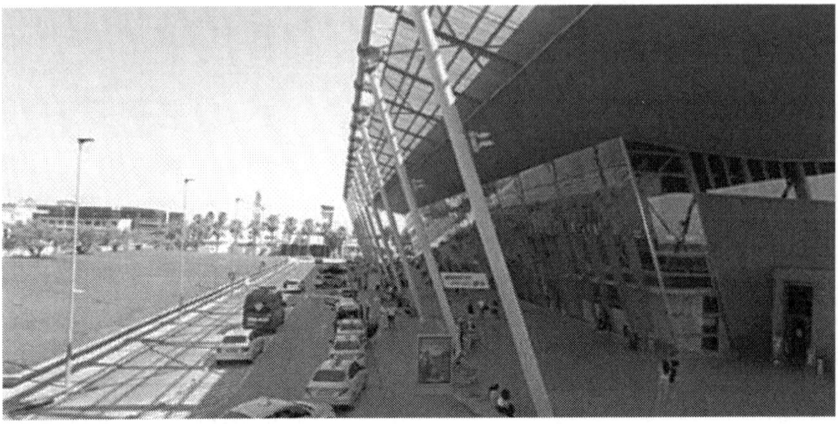

Table of Contents

Introduction — 8
- Why Experience Tirana Like a Local? — 10
- How to Use This Guide — 12

Chapter 1: — 15
Getting Acquainted with Tirana — 15
- A Brief History of Tirana — 15
- The Modern Landscape of Tirana — 17
- Local Culture and Traditions — 20

Chapter 2: — 23
Navigating Tirana's Neighborhoods — 23
- Blloku: Trendy Hotspot — 23
- Skanderbeg Square: Heart of the City — 25
- Pazari i Ri: The New Bazaar — 28
- Tanners' Bridge Area: Where Past Meets Present — 30
- Lana River Embankment: Serene Strolls — 33

Chapter 3 — 37
Unveiling Hidden Gems — 37
- BunkArt: Cold War Relics — 37
- Petrela Castle: A Glimpse into the Past — 40
- Grand Park (Parku i Madh): Nature Oasis — 42
- Cave of Pellumbas: Subterranean Adventure — 45
- Komiteti Café: Nostalgic Vibes — 47

Chapter 4 — 51
Essential Sights and Landmarks — 51
- Et'hem Bey Mosque: Architectural Marvel — 51
- National History Museum: Stories of the Past — 54

- Pyramid of Tirana: Controversial Icon   56
- Dajti Mountain: Panoramic Views   59
- Clock Tower: Ascend Through Time   62

Chapter 5   65
Embracing Tirana's Culinary Scene   65
- Albanian Gastronomy: An Overview   65
- Top Traditional Dishes to Try   68
- Best Local Eateries and Restaurants   74
- Savoring Budget-Friendly Delights: Where to Enjoy Delectable Eats   76
- International Cuisine in Tirana   78
- Tirana's Coffee Culture   80
- Sweet Delights: Desserts and Pastries   83

Chapter 6   87
Immersing in Local Experiences   87
- Attending Festivals and Events   87
- Art and Music Scene of Tirana   91
- Shopping in Bazaars and Boutiques   93
- Enjoying Tirana's Nightlife   96
- Connecting with Locals: Language and Etiquette   99

Chapter 7   105
Day Trips and Excursions   105
- Kruja: Historical Day Trip   105
- Durres: Sun, Sea, and History   107
- Berat: City of a Thousand Windows   110
- Shkodra: Where History and Nature Converge   113
- Theth: Alpine Adventure   115

Chapter 8   119
Practical Information   119

- Getting to Tirana 119
- Getting Around the City 122
- Accommodation Options 125
- Safety Tips and Emergency Contacts 128
- Useful Phrases for Travelers 130
- Conversion Charts and Measurements 132
- Dress Comfortably and Stylishly in Vibrant Tirana! 133

Conclusion **137**
Bonus Chapter **139**
Tirana Travel Journal **139**

Introduction

Welcome to Tirana!

Hey there, fellow adventurers! Are you ready to embark on a journey that will lead you to the heart of an enchanting city? Well, look no further, because I'm here to regale you with tales of Tirana, a place that's more than just a city – it's a vibrant tapestry of culture, history, and flavor that's waiting to be unraveled.

Imagine this: a city where the past and present waltz together in perfect harmony, where the air is filled with the laughter of locals, and the streets are alive with the buzz of excitement. That's Tirana for you, a city that I've come to adore like an old friend.

As you step foot on the cobblestone streets, you'll feel the beating heart of Tirana. You'll be swept away by the rhythm of life, the colorful buildings standing shoulder to shoulder, and the warm smiles of its people. It's a place where tradition meets innovation, where history is celebrated, and where every corner holds a story waiting to be shared.

Now, let me tell you – experiencing Tirana like a local is the key to truly unlocking its magic. Sure, you could stick to the well-trodden tourist paths, but why not go beyond that? Immerse yourself in the local neighborhoods, savor the tantalizing flavors of authentic Albanian cuisine, and discover hidden gems that aren't on the typical travel brochures.Throughout this guide, I'll be your storyteller, your guide to the uncharted alleys, the must-visit sights, and the tantalizing culinary delights that await you. I'll share with you the nooks and crannies that have stolen my heart, the local secrets that have made me fall head over heels for Tirana.

So, whether you're a history buff seeking ancient treasures, a foodie eager to explore new tastes, an art enthusiast in search of creativity, or simply a traveler hungry for new experiences, Tirana has something to offer you. It's a city that welcomes you with open arms, inviting you to create your own memories and stories within its vibrant streets.Get ready to immerse yourself in the rhythm of life, to taste the flavors of tradition, and to uncover the city's best-kept secrets. Your adventure in Tirana begins now, and I'm thrilled to be your companion on this joyous journey of discovery. So, my fellow travelers, let's dive into the heart and soul of Tirana and experience it like the locals do – with open hearts, curious minds, and boundless excitement.

- Why Experience Tirana Like a Local?

When you're planning your travel itinerary, it's easy to get caught up in the whirlwind of tourist attractions and popular landmarks. But if you truly want to uncover the soul of a city, there's no better way than to experience it like a local. And when it comes to Tirana, this approach isn't just a suggestion – it's a gateway to a richer, more authentic exploration. Here's why immersing yourself in Tirana as a local is the ultimate way to discover its true essence:

1. Unearth Hidden Gems: Locals hold the key to the city's best-kept secrets. Those charming alleyways, tucked-away cafes, and scenic spots that might not make it to the front page of a travel guide? Locals know them well. By tapping into their knowledge, you'll discover places that aren't overrun by crowds, allowing you to experience the city's magic in tranquility.

2. Embrace Authentic Culture: The heart of any city lies in its culture, and the best way to truly understand it is by engaging with the locals. From participating in traditional festivals to mingling with artisans in local markets, you'll gain insights into the customs, traditions, and way of life that define Tirana. It's a chance to bridge the gap between being a spectator and becoming a part of the tapestry.

3. Taste the True Flavors: Tirana's culinary scene is a treasure trove of flavors waiting to be discovered. While restaurants geared toward tourists offer a taste of the local cuisine, it's often the unassuming eateries and family-owned establishments where you'll find the most authentic dishes. Engage with locals to get recommendations, and you'll find yourself savoring traditional recipes that have been passed down through generations.

4. Connect on a Personal Level: The people of Tirana are known for their warmth and hospitality. By interacting with locals, you'll not only create meaningful connections but also gain a deeper understanding of their perspectives, challenges, and aspirations. Conversations with Tirana's residents can be as enlightening as they are heartwarming, leaving you with lasting memories.

5. Navigate with Confidence: Navigating a new city can be intimidating, but having a local perspective can make all the difference. Locals can provide valuable insights on transportation options, safety tips, and cultural norms, ensuring that you experience Tirana smoothly and with confidence.

6. Contribute to Sustainable Tourism: When you choose to experience Tirana like a local, you're supporting the local economy in a more direct and sustainable way. Your spending benefits small businesses, artisans, and communities, helping to preserve the city's unique character for generations to come.

In a world where travel has the power to connect people and cultures, experiencing Tirana like a local isn't just a way to explore a new destination — it's a way to enrich your own journey and leave with a deeper appreciation for the city and its people. So, as you plan your adventure, remember that the best stories and memories often come from stepping off the beaten path and immersing yourself in the authentic rhythm of Tirana.

- How to Use This Guide

Welcome to the "Tirana Travel Guide 2023: A Pocket size Enticing Guide to Exploring the beauty of Tirana like a Local." This guide has been crafted to help you make the most of your journey through the vibrant streets and hidden corners of Tirana. Whether you're a first-time visitor or returning for another adventure, here's how to navigate and make the most of this guide:

1. Chapter Navigation: Each chapter is designed to take you on a journey through a specific aspect of Tirana, from its history and neighborhoods to its culinary scene and local experiences. To find information on a particular topic, refer to the table of contents to quickly locate the relevant chapter.

2. Subsections and Headings: Each chapter is divided into subsections and headings that address specific areas or topics. This structure allows you to find information that interests you most. Simply skim the headings to locate the information you're seeking.

3. Maps and Visual References: To help you navigate Tirana's streets and attractions, this guide includes maps and visual references. These visual aids will help you gain a better understanding of the city's layout and the locations of key points of interest.

4. Recommendations and Tips: Look out for recommendations, tips, and insider insights from locals and experienced travelers. These tidbits of information can enhance your experience and offer valuable guidance.

5. Practical Information: At the end of the guide, you'll find practical information sections, including details on getting to Tirana, transportation options, accommodation, safety tips, and more. These sections are designed to assist you in planning and enjoying a smooth and comfortable trip.

6. Personalization: Remember that your journey is unique, and while this guide provides comprehensive information, feel free to tailor your exploration to your interests and preferences. Use the guide as a foundation, but don't hesitate to deviate and discover your own hidden treasures.

As you flip through these pages and delve into the wonders of Tirana, keep in mind that travel is about embracing the unknown, stepping out of your comfort zone, and embracing the beauty of a new place. Let this guide be your companion, offering insights and stories to enrich your experience in Tirana. With an open heart and a curious spirit, embark on your adventure and make lasting memories in this remarkable city.

Chapter 1:

Getting Acquainted with Tirana

- A Brief History of Tirana

Nestled in the heart of Albania, Tirana's history is as diverse and captivating as the city itself. From its humble beginnings as a small settlement to its present-day status as the vibrant capital, Tirana's journey through time is marked by the footsteps of various civilizations and the indomitable spirit of its people.

Ancient Foundations:
Tirana's history traces back to ancient times, when Illyrian tribes inhabited the region. These early settlers established a small settlement in the area, drawn by the fertile land and strategic location. The Romans later recognized the potential of this site and established a trading post known as Theranda.

Medieval Shifts:
With the fall of the Roman Empire, the region experienced shifts in power and cultural influence.

Byzantine, Slavic, and Ottoman forces vied for control, leaving their architectural and cultural imprints on the evolving city. During the Ottoman rule, Tirana gradually transformed into a bustling center for trade and craftsmanship.

Emergence as a Capital:
Tirana's trajectory changed dramatically with Albania's declaration of independence in 1912. The city was chosen as the capital due to its central location and potential for growth. This marked a significant turning point, as Tirana shifted from a provincial town to the seat of national governance.

Communist Era:
The mid-20th century ushered in a new era as Albania fell under communist rule led by Enver Hoxha. This period saw extensive urban planning, as grand boulevards and monumental structures were erected to portray the regime's power. While these constructions left a distinct mark on the cityscape, they also reflected a darker chapter in Tirana's history.

Transition to Democracy:
Following the fall of communism in 1990, Tirana underwent a profound transformation. The city embraced newfound freedoms, leading to an explosion of creativity and cultural expression. Brightly painted buildings, street art, and a burgeoning arts scene breathed new life into the city, setting the stage for its contemporary identity.

Modern Vibrancy:
Today, Tirana stands as a city that deftly blends its rich history with modern influences. The past is evident in the mosaic of architectural styles that grace its streets, from Ottoman mosques to socialist-era buildings. Yet, it's the city's resilience and determination to embrace progress that define its present spirit.

Tirana's history is a tapestry woven from the threads of conquerors, empires, and ideologies. It's a city that has faced challenges head-on, emerging with a vibrant culture, welcoming locals, and a unique charm that draws visitors from around the world. As you explore Tirana's streets and landmarks, remember that you're walking in the footsteps of countless generations, each contributing to the captivating story that defines this remarkable capital.

- The Modern Landscape of Tirana

As the capital of Albania, Tirana has transformed itself into a dynamic hub of modernity while retaining its historical essence. With a captivating blend of contemporary architecture, bustling neighborhoods, and a thriving cultural scene, Tirana's modern landscape paints a picture of a city that is constantly evolving and embracing change.

Architectural Diversity:
Tirana's architecture is a testament to its journey through time. The cityscape showcases an eclectic mix of styles, ranging from Ottoman-era structures to stark communist-era buildings and cutting-edge contemporary designs. You'll find ornate mosques standing alongside sleek glass skyscrapers, creating a captivating visual contrast that tells the story of Tirana's history and progress.

Colorful Transformation:
One of the most visually striking features of modern Tirana is its vibrant and colorful facades. As a symbol of the city's transition from communism to freedom, many buildings have shed their drab gray exteriors in favor of bold and bright colors. Walking through the streets, you'll be treated to a kaleidoscope of hues that reflect the optimism and creativity of the city's residents.

Green Spaces and Parks:
Tirana's modern landscape also emphasizes the importance of green spaces. The city boasts a number of well-maintained parks and gardens that provide a welcome respite from the urban bustle. Grand Park (Parku i Madh), for instance, offers locals and visitors a chance to escape into nature, with walking paths, lakes, and recreational facilities.

Cultural Renaissance:

The past few decades have witnessed a cultural renaissance in Tirana, with a renewed emphasis on the arts, music, and creative expression. The city is home to numerous art galleries, museums, and performance venues that showcase both local and international talent. From contemporary art exhibitions to traditional music festivals, Tirana's cultural scene is a vibrant tapestry of creativity.

Cafés and Urban Hangouts:
Tirana's urban landscape is dotted with trendy cafés, stylish bars, and inviting public spaces where locals and visitors gather to socialize, work, or simply soak in the city's energy. The Blloku neighborhood, once restricted to high-ranking officials during communist rule, has transformed into a lively district filled with eateries, shops, and a lively nightlife.

Inclusive Atmosphere:
One of the hallmarks of modern Tirana is its inclusive atmosphere. The city embraces diversity and welcomes people from all walks of life. This openness is reflected in the wide range of cultural events, festivals, and celebrations that take place throughout the year, celebrating different traditions and fostering unity among its residents.Tirana's modern landscape is a reflection of its people's resilience, creativity, and forward-thinking spirit. It's a city that has not only embraced change but has also celebrated it, weaving the threads of history into a vibrant tapestry of contemporary life. As you explore the streets, parks, and cultural venues, you'll

experience the modern essence of Tirana — a city that stands as a shining example of progress while honoring its past.

- Local Culture and Traditions

In the heart of Tirana, the pulse of local culture and traditions beats rhythmically, creating a tapestry of identity that is both unique and deeply rooted in history. As you immerse yourself in the city's vibrant streets and engage with its welcoming residents, you'll uncover a rich blend of customs, celebrations, and practices that showcase Tirana's sense of community and pride.

Hospitality and Warmth:
Hospitality is a cornerstone of Tirana's culture. Locals are known for their warmth and genuine friendliness, often going out of their way to make visitors feel at home. A simple gesture like sharing a cup of coffee with a stranger can quickly turn into a heartwarming connection that exemplifies the city's open and inviting atmosphere.

Language and Communication:
While Albanian is the official language, many Tirana residents also speak English, especially in urban areas. Taking the time to learn a few basic Albanian phrases can go a long way in showing respect for the local

culture and engaging in meaningful interactions with the people you meet.

Family and Community:
Family holds immense importance in Tirana's culture. Extended families often live in close proximity and gather regularly to celebrate special occasions and maintain strong bonds. Community events, festivals, and religious holidays also bring people together, reinforcing the sense of unity that runs through the city's veins.

Religious Harmony:
Tirana is a shining example of religious harmony, with a diverse mix of faiths peacefully coexisting. Mosques, churches, and other religious sites dot the cityscape, reflecting the acceptance and mutual respect that define the local ethos. Visitors are welcome to explore these sites and gain insights into the spiritual aspects of Tirana's culture.

Artistic Expression:
Art and creativity are integral to Tirana's cultural fabric. The city is a canvas for street artists who use their craft to convey messages of hope, reflection, and social commentary. Additionally, Tirana's galleries and performance spaces showcase a wide range of artistic expressions, from traditional to contemporary.

Festivals and Celebrations:

Tirana comes alive with vibrant festivals and celebrations that honor both national and local traditions. Festivals like Dita e Verës (Summer Day) and Dita e Flamurit (Flag Day) are marked by lively parades, performances, and cultural displays. These events offer a glimpse into the heart of Tirana's heritage and the pride its residents take in their roots.

Culinary Traditions:
Tirana's culinary scene is a testament to the city's cultural diversity. Traditional Albanian dishes, often centered around fresh ingredients and simple preparation, hold a special place on local tables. Exploring the city's markets, cafés, and restaurants allows you to savor the flavors that have been passed down through generations.

As you engage with the local culture and traditions of Tirana, you'll discover that the city's beauty lies not only in its landmarks and architecture but also in the rich tapestry of customs that shape its identity. Embrace the spirit of community, celebrate alongside locals, and take part in the timeless rituals that make Tirana an enchanting destination where history and modernity seamlessly intertwine.

Chapter 2:

Navigating Tirana's Neighborhoods

- Blloku: Trendy Hotspot

Nestled in the heart of Tirana, Blloku emerges as a vibrant neighborhood that encapsulates the city's transformation from the past to the present. Once a restricted area during communist rule, Blloku has evolved into a trendy hotspot that encapsulates the spirit of Tirana's modern culture and cosmopolitan energy.

A Historical Evolution:
Blloku, short for "Blok" (Block), was once a residential area reserved for high-ranking communist officials. During that era, it was off-limits to the general public. However, following the fall of communism, Blloku underwent a remarkable transformation, shedding its exclusive status to become a symbol of Albania's transition to democracy.

Cafés and Culinary Delights:
Today, Blloku is synonymous with a lively café culture and a plethora of dining options. Its streets are lined with chic cafés, eateries, and bars that spill out onto the

sidewalks, creating an inviting atmosphere for both locals and visitors. From traditional Albanian fare to international cuisine, Blloku's culinary scene caters to a diverse range of tastes.

Shopping and Boutiques:
Blloku also offers a shopping experience that blends modernity with traditional craftsmanship. Boutiques and shops showcase local designers, artists, and artisans, allowing you to discover unique fashion, accessories, and souvenirs that capture the essence of Tirana's creative spirit.

Nightlife and Entertainment:
As the sun sets, Blloku transforms into a bustling nightlife hub. The district's bars and clubs come alive with music, dancing, and a vibrant energy that attracts revelers from all corners of the city. Whether you're in the mood for live music, DJ sets, or simply mingling with locals, Blloku offers a range of options for a memorable night out.

Art and Expression:
Blloku's walls tell stories through vibrant street art and graffiti. The neighborhood's artistic expression mirrors the city's journey from a history-laden past to a modern, forward-thinking present. The streets themselves become an open-air gallery, reflecting the dynamic fusion of Tirana's heritage and contemporary influences.

A Symbol of Transformation:
Blloku's transformation is not just physical; it's a reflection of Albania's transition from a closed society to an open and vibrant democracy. The district stands as a testament to the resilience of the Albanian people, who have embraced change and created a space that embodies the city's progressive spirit.

Embrace the Essence:
Exploring Blloku offers a glimpse into Tirana's multifaceted identity. It's a place where history, culture, and modernity seamlessly converge, inviting you to immerse yourself in the dynamic atmosphere that defines the city today. So, whether you're sipping coffee at a sidewalk café, discovering local art, or dancing the night away, Blloku beckons you to experience Tirana's heartbeat in one of its most dynamic and trendsetting neighborhoods.

- Skanderbeg Square: Heart of the City

At the center of Tirana's urban pulse lies the iconic Skanderbeg Square, a sprawling open space that serves as the heartbeat of the city. Named after the national hero, Gjergj Kastrioti Skanderbeg, this square is not just a physical landmark; it's a symbolic hub that encapsulates Tirana's history, culture, and modern vitality.

A Historical Nexus:
Skanderbeg Square's significance reaches far back in time. It was once a bustling bazaar during the Ottoman era, a testament to Tirana's historical trading importance. Over the years, the square witnessed shifts in governance and ideologies, reflecting the changing tides of the city's story.

Iconic Landmarks:
Surrounded by an eclectic mix of architectural styles, Skanderbeg Square boasts several notable landmarks. The National History Museum stands as a prominent edifice, housing artifacts that narrate Albania's historical journey. The Et'hem Bey Mosque, with its intricate frescoes and elegant minaret, showcases Tirana's spiritual and architectural heritage.

Public Gathering Space:
Skanderbeg Square is more than just a historical site; it's a vibrant public gathering space that comes alive with events, celebrations, and everyday life. Locals and visitors alike congregate here to meet friends, people-watch, and partake in the rhythm of the city. The square's spaciousness invites leisurely strolls, picnics, and a sense of community.

Cultural and Political Hub:
Skanderbeg Square has been the stage for countless cultural events, rallies, and national celebrations. Its role as a gathering point for political demonstrations and rallies during pivotal moments in Albania's history

speaks to its significance as a space where the voice of the people echoes.

Modern Renovation:
In recent years, Skanderbeg Square underwent a transformation that revitalized its identity. The square's redesign prioritized pedestrian access, creating a pedestrian-friendly environment that invites exploration. Modern fountains, artistic installations, and green spaces were introduced, striking a balance between historical preservation and contemporary urban planning.

A Tapestry of Tirana:
Skanderbeg Square is a reflection of Tirana's resilience and evolution. Its layers of history, cultural events, and architectural styles come together to form a vibrant tapestry that represents the city's spirit. Whether you're admiring the statues, enjoying a cup of coffee at a nearby café, or simply basking in the energy of the square, you're becoming a part of the ongoing story that Skanderbeg Square embodies.

An Emblem of Unity:
Skanderbeg Square stands as a unifying symbol, bridging the gap between Tirana's past and present. It's a place where history mingles with the contemporary, where diverse stories converge, and where Tirana's heart beats in harmony with its people. As you explore this urban oasis, remember that you're treading upon

hallowed ground that connects you to the essence of the city itself.

- Pazari i Ri: The New Bazaar

In the heart of Tirana, a vibrant marketplace awaits, offering a delightful blend of tradition and modernity – Pazari i Ri, also known as the New Bazaar. This bustling hub of commerce, flavors, and culture embodies Tirana's spirit of evolution while paying homage to its rich historical roots.

A Market with History:
Pazari i Ri's origins date back to the 17th century when it was established as a bustling Ottoman-era market. Over the years, it has been a focal point for trade, bringing together merchants, artisans, and customers from all walks of life. Today, while its essence remains true to its origins, it has undergone a transformation that embraces contemporary trends.

Culinary Exploration:
The heart and soul of Pazari i Ri lie in its culinary offerings. Stroll through its lively alleys and be captivated by the aromas of freshly baked bread, local cheeses, spices, and an array of colorful produce. From traditional Albanian specialties to international flavors, this market is a gastronomic haven that invites you to savor authentic tastes.

Fresh and Local:
Pazari i Ri is renowned for its emphasis on fresh, locally sourced products. Farmers from nearby villages gather here to display their harvest, creating a direct link between the rural landscapes and the city's urban life. This commitment to supporting local producers is a testament to the market's role in fostering community ties.

Craftsmanship and Culture:
Beyond its culinary delights, Pazari i Ri showcases a variety of crafts and goods. Artisans offer intricately woven textiles, handmade ceramics, traditional clothing, and unique souvenirs that reflect Albania's cultural heritage. Exploring the market's stalls is like embarking on a journey through the country's craftsmanship and creativity.

The New Bazaar Revival:
Pazari i Ri has experienced a renaissance in recent years, with careful renovations that honor its history while introducing modern conveniences. The market now boasts a combination of open-air stalls, covered sections, and a mix of traditional and contemporary architecture, creating an inviting and comfortable environment for both locals and visitors.

Gathering Place:
Pazari i Ri is more than just a market; it's a meeting place where locals come to connect, share stories, and enjoy the sense of community that has characterized

Tirana for generations. As you navigate its vibrant corridors and interact with vendors, you'll witness the genuine warmth and hospitality that define Albanian culture.

A Window into Tirana:
Pazari i Ri offers a window into the heart of Tirana – a city that embraces change while remaining deeply connected to its heritage. It's a microcosm of the city's journey, a place where old and new harmoniously coexist. So, whether you're shopping for local delicacies, seeking unique crafts, or simply soaking in the lively atmosphere, Pazari i Ri invites you to experience the timeless allure of Tirana's marketscape.

- Tanners' Bridge Area: Where Past Meets Present

Step into a picturesque corner of Tirana where the threads of history intertwine with the pulse of modern life – the Tanners' Bridge Area. This charming district is a living testament to the city's evolution, inviting you to wander through cobblestone streets, explore cultural landmarks, and experience the seamless blend of old-world charm and contemporary energy.

Historical Echoes:
The heart of the Tanners' Bridge Area is, unsurprisingly, the Tanners' Bridge itself – a centuries-old stone bridge that once served as a crucial link across the Lana River.

This area, with its cobbled streets and restored buildings, harks back to a time when Tirana was a small town defined by its artisans and tradesmen.

Artisan Legacy:
In centuries past, the Tanners' Bridge Area was a hub for leatherworking, where skilled artisans crafted leather goods that were sought after throughout the region. Although the leather industry has given way to modernization, the district retains its historical charm, serving as a reminder of Tirana's humble beginnings.

Modern Revival:
While steeped in history, the Tanners' Bridge Area has experienced a revival that celebrates both its past and its present. The area's restoration efforts have breathed new life into its architecture, transforming old buildings into vibrant cafés, galleries, and shops that cater to a modern audience while preserving the district's authentic character.

Cultural Enclaves:
As you explore the Tanners' Bridge Area, you'll encounter an array of cultural treasures. Galleries and craft shops showcase the work of local artists, while quaint cafés invite you to savor a cup of coffee and absorb the surroundings. The district's cultural spaces provide a platform for creativity to flourish in the heart of Tirana.

Historical Landmarks:

Beyond the Tanners' Bridge, the area is home to a collection of historical landmarks that shed light on Tirana's journey. The nearby Ethnographic Museum offers insights into Albanian traditions and heritage, while the Saint Procopius Church stands as a testament to the city's spiritual history.

Local Spirit:
The Tanners' Bridge Area encapsulates Tirana's unique sense of community and neighborly connection. As you walk its streets, you'll encounter friendly faces, engage in conversations with locals, and feel the genuine warmth that characterizes the city. The district invites you to not only explore its attractions but also engage with its people.

A Living Tapestry:
The Tanners' Bridge Area isn't just a snapshot of Tirana's past – it's a living, breathing tapestry that weaves together history and modernity. It's a place where you can lose yourself in the ambiance of yesteryears while being surrounded by the energy of a vibrant city.

Immersive Experience:
Visiting the Tanners' Bridge Area offers more than just sightseeing; it's an opportunity to step into the intricate narrative of Tirana's evolution. It's a reminder that while cities change, the stories they hold are etched into their very foundations, waiting to be discovered by those who wander its streets with curiosity and appreciation.

- Lana River Embankment: Serene Strolls

Tucked away from the city's hustle and bustle, the Lana River Embankment offers a tranquil escape where nature's beauty meets urban serenity. This charming pathway follows the gentle meander of the Lana River, providing a scenic retreat that invites both locals and visitors to unwind, take leisurely strolls, and find solace in the midst of Tirana's vibrant energy.

Nature's Respite:
The Lana River Embankment is a sanctuary for those seeking a break from the urban pace. Lined with trees, shrubs, and green spaces, the pathway offers a refreshing dose of nature within the heart of the city. The soothing sound of flowing water and the rustle of leaves create an ambiance that calms the senses.

Scenic Vistas:
As you amble along the embankment, you'll be treated to picturesque views that paint a peaceful scene. The river's gentle flow, the lush foliage, and the occasional glimpse of swans gracefully gliding on the water all contribute to an atmosphere of serenity that feels far removed from the urban hustle.

Leisurely Exploration:
The Lana River Embankment beckons you to take leisurely walks and savor the moment. Whether you're walking alone, sharing a conversation with a friend, or simply enjoying your own thoughts, this pathway

provides a setting that encourages mindfulness and reflection.

Artistic Touches:
The embankment also serves as a canvas for artistic expression. Alongside the pathway, you'll encounter sculptures, installations, and artistic creations that add an element of creativity to your stroll. These subtle touches enhance the overall experience, making each step a journey of discovery.

Bridge to Connectivity:
Several pedestrian bridges connect both sides of the Lana River, fostering connectivity and allowing you to explore the city's neighborhoods. Crossing these bridges provides new vantage points and a deeper appreciation for Tirana's unique layout.

Local Flavor:
The Lana River Embankment isn't just a place for nature enthusiasts; it's also an integral part of local life. Families gather for picnics, couples stroll hand in hand, and joggers and cyclists make use of the pathway to stay active. This mingling of residents and visitors creates a sense of community within the serene backdrop.

A Breath of Fresh Air:
Whether you're seeking a quiet escape, a picturesque setting for photography, or simply a breath of fresh air, the Lana River Embankment offers it all. It's a reminder

that amidst the urban excitement, Tirana treasures its pockets of tranquility, inviting you to slow down and appreciate the simple pleasures of life.

Unwind and Recharge:
The Lana River Embankment beckons with open arms, inviting you to step away from the city's hustle and immerse yourself in its calming embrace. It's a reminder that amidst the vibrant urban tapestry of Tirana, moments of serenity await those who seek them along the gentle flow of the Lana River.

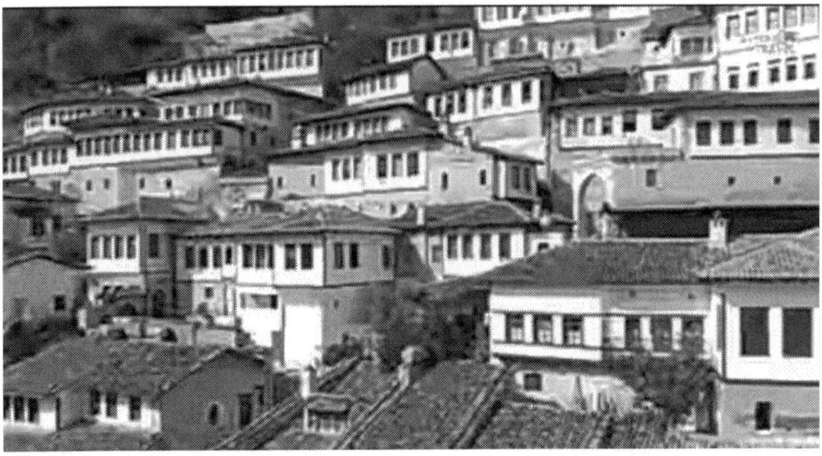

Chapter 3

Unveiling Hidden Gems

- BunkArt: Cold War Relics

Nestled within the heart of Tirana lies a thought-provoking journey into Albania's tumultuous past – BunkArt. This unique museum, housed in a massive underground bunker, offers a captivating glimpse into the era of the Cold War, providing visitors with a haunting reminder of the city's history during a time of isolation and uncertainty.

A Hidden Fortress:
BunkArt is situated within a vast underground bunker complex that was built during the rule of Enver Hoxha, Albania's former communist leader. This secret facility, designed to serve as a shelter for high-ranking officials, remained shrouded in mystery until its transformation into a museum.

Time Capsule of History:
Stepping into BunkArt is like stepping back in time. The museum meticulously preserves the bunker's original architecture and features, allowing visitors to experience the stark reality of life during Albania's isolated and

authoritarian years. From narrow corridors to cramped chambers, the space itself becomes a vessel of historical reflection.

Visual Narratives:
BunkArt's exhibitions provide a comprehensive narrative of Albania's Cold War history. Through photographs, documents, artifacts, and multimedia displays, visitors gain insights into the regime's propaganda, surveillance methods, and the lives of those affected by its policies. The museum doesn't shy away from presenting the complexities and harsh realities of the past.

Stories of Survival:
As you explore BunkArt, you'll encounter stories of ordinary Albanians who navigated life under strict government control. Personal accounts of defiance, resilience, and survival shed light on the human spirit's capacity to endure even in the face of adversity.

Artistic Interpretations:
In addition to its historical exhibitions, BunkArt also features artistic installations that provide a unique perspective on the Cold War era. These thought-provoking artworks engage visitors in discussions about the impact of political ideologies and the importance of safeguarding freedom.

Reckoning with the Past:
BunkArt serves as a poignant reminder of Tirana's journey from isolation to openness. It's a space where

the past confronts the present, encouraging visitors to reflect on the significance of preserving historical memory and safeguarding democratic values.

Educational Insight:
BunkArt is not just a museum; it's an educational experience that deepens your understanding of Albania's history. Whether you're a history enthusiast, a curious traveler, or someone seeking a better grasp of the global impact of the Cold War, BunkArt offers an immersive learning opportunity.

Honoring Resilience:
Above all, BunkArt pays tribute to the resilience of the Albanian people who emerged from a period of darkness into a new era of hope and progress. It's a testament to the power of remembrance and the importance of understanding the past as a means of shaping a brighter future.

A Journey of Reflection:
BunkArt isn't just a museum – it's an emotional journey that prompts reflection on the complexities of history, ideology, and human perseverance. As you explore the depths of this Cold War relic, you'll find yourself grappling with the challenges of a bygone era while drawing parallels to the world we live in today.

- Petrela Castle: A Glimpse into the Past

High atop a hill, overlooking the picturesque landscape surrounding Tirana, stands Petrela Castle – a timeless sentinel that offers a captivating journey back in time. This historic fortress, with its ancient walls, panoramic views, and storied past, invites you to explore Albania's rich history while basking in the beauty of the present.

Majestic Vantage Point:
Perched on a hill approximately 15 kilometers from Tirana, Petrela Castle commands breathtaking views of the rolling hills, valleys, and distant mountains. Its strategic location once made it a crucial defensive post, allowing its inhabitants to monitor the surrounding landscape and safeguard their territory.

Ancient Origins:
Petrela Castle's origins trace back to antiquity, with traces of Illyrian and Roman settlements in its vicinity. The castle itself was established during the Byzantine era and later expanded by the Ottomans. Its layered history is evident in the mix of architectural styles that have shaped its structure.

Defensive Legacy:
Throughout its history, Petrela Castle played a vital role in defending its inhabitants from various threats. Its robust walls, watchtowers, and battlements stand as a

testament to the fortress's strategic importance in an age of shifting powers and territorial disputes.

Exploring the Ruins:
As you wander through the castle's ruins, you'll encounter remnants of its past – from medieval stone archways to worn staircases and chambers that once housed soldiers and residents. The sense of stepping back in time is palpable, as each stone and wall carries the weight of centuries.

A Scenic Retreat:
Petrela Castle not only immerses you in history but also offers a peaceful retreat from the modern world. The castle's surroundings provide ample opportunities for leisurely walks, picnics, and contemplation, allowing you to connect with nature while marveling at the ancient architecture.

Local Legends:
The castle is shrouded in folklore and legends that add a layer of mystery to its narrative. Stories of heroism, romance, and intrigue have been passed down through generations, adding an element of enchantment to the experience of visiting this historic site.

Cultural Heritage:
Petrela Castle stands as a symbol of Albania's cultural heritage, a living monument that testifies to the resilience of its people throughout history. Its

significance extends beyond its architectural beauty; it embodies the nation's journey through time.

A Timeless Tale:
Visiting Petrela Castle offers more than just a historical experience; it's a journey that bridges the past with the present. As you explore the castle's nooks and crannies, you become a part of its story, a traveler who has walked the same paths as those who came before.

Capturing the Imagination:
Petrela Castle captures the imagination and invites you to contemplate the lives, struggles, and triumphs of those who once called it home. It's a place where history comes alive, where you can pause to reflect on the passage of time while admiring the beauty that has endured for centuries.

- Grand Park (Parku i Madh): Nature Oasis

Amidst the bustling urban landscape of Tirana, a verdant haven awaits – the Grand Park, affectionately known as "Parku i Madh." This sprawling natural oasis offers a tranquil escape from the city's energy, inviting you to immerse yourself in lush greenery, serene lakes, and a variety of recreational activities.

A Tranquil Retreat:
Grand Park is a sanctuary where nature takes center stage. Its expansive lawns, shaded pathways, and serene atmosphere create an ideal setting for leisurely strolls, picnics, and moments of introspection. The park's serene ambiance allows visitors to temporarily disconnect from the urban tempo.

Natural Splendor:
As you explore the park's winding trails, you'll encounter a rich tapestry of flora and fauna. Towering trees, vibrant blooms, and diverse bird species inhabit the park, providing a haven for both wildlife and those seeking solace in nature's embrace.

Lakeside Serenity:
The park's centerpiece is its serene lake, a tranquil expanse of water where you can unwind by its shores or take a leisurely boat ride. The gentle ripples of the water and the surrounding greenery create a picturesque scene that feels worlds away from the city's hustle.

Recreational Opportunities:
Grand Park offers a range of recreational activities for visitors of all ages. From jogging and cycling along dedicated paths to open spaces for sports and yoga, the park caters to those seeking active pursuits amidst the natural backdrop.

Cultural and Artistic Touches:
Within the park, you'll also find cultural and artistic elements that enrich the experience. Sculptures, art installations, and event spaces contribute to the park's multifaceted identity, infusing creativity into the natural landscape.

Community Gathering:
Grand Park is more than just a green space; it's a place where the community gathers. Families enjoy quality time together, friends meet for leisurely conversations, and cultural events often take place on its open lawns, creating a sense of unity and connection.

Escape into Serenity:
Whether you're seeking a place to read a book under the shade of a tree, go for a jog to clear your mind, or simply sit by the water and watch the world go by, Grand Park offers an inviting canvas for relaxation and rejuvenation.

Balance of Urban and Natural:
Grand Park's existence within a bustling city is a testament to Tirana's commitment to preserving green spaces for its residents and visitors. It's a reminder that amidst urban expansion, the importance of natural retreats remains paramount.

Harmony with Nature:
Visiting Grand Park is more than just experiencing a picturesque setting; it's an opportunity to reconnect with

the rhythms of nature, to find balance amidst the urban chaos, and to appreciate the serenity that unfolds when humans and the natural world coexist harmoniously.

- Cave of Pellumbas: Subterranean Adventure

Beneath the rugged terrain surrounding Tirana lies a hidden marvel waiting to be explored – the Cave of Pellumbas. This captivating subterranean wonderland offers an exhilarating adventure for those who seek to journey deep into the earth, uncovering geological wonders and immersing themselves in the mysteries of the underground realm.

Nature's Spectacle:
The Cave of Pellumbas is a testament to the forces of nature that shape our world. Over millions of years, water and time have sculpted intricate formations within its chambers, creating a mesmerizing display of stalactites, stalagmites, and other unique features that adorn its walls and ceilings.

A Voyage Underground:
Descending into the cave is like stepping into a different realm altogether. Guided by the soft glow of your flashlight, you'll traverse narrow passages, navigate through chambers of varying sizes, and witness the mesmerizing interplay of light and shadow that dance upon the cave's formations.

Geological Tapestry:
The cave's interior offers an unparalleled geological tapestry, showcasing the intricate processes that shaped its unique features. Stalactites drip like frozen raindrops from above, while stalagmites rise from the ground, creating an otherworldly landscape that sparks the imagination.

Ancient History:
The Cave of Pellumbas isn't just a geological wonder; it's also a repository of ancient history. Archaeological findings within the cave provide insights into its past use by humans and animals. As you explore its depths, you'll connect with the generations that once sought refuge within its cool embrace.

Awe-Inspiring Atmosphere:
The silence and darkness of the cave create an atmosphere that is simultaneously humbling and awe-inspiring. The sense of wonder that accompanies each step adds an element of adventure and discovery to the experience.

Adventurous Spirit:
Exploring the Cave of Pellumbas requires an adventurous spirit. You'll navigate uneven terrain, marvel at the natural formations, and perhaps even catch glimpses of cave-dwelling creatures that have adapted to life in this unique environment.

An Encounter with Nature:
Visiting the Cave of Pellumbas is not just an adventure; it's an intimate encounter with the natural world. It's a chance to witness the Earth's geological history up close, to connect with the forces that shaped the landscape, and to appreciate the wonders that lie hidden beneath the surface.

A Journey of Discovery:
Descending into the Cave of Pellumbas is more than just exploring an underground wonder; it's a journey of discovery that ignites curiosity and sparks a deeper connection with the natural world. As you emerge from the depths, you'll carry with you not only memories of the adventure but also a newfound appreciation for the Earth's secrets that lie beneath our feet.

- Komiteti Café: Nostalgic Vibes

Nestled in the heart of Tirana, Komiteti Café is a charming establishment that takes you on a delightful journey back in time. Stepping into this café is like stepping into the past, as it effortlessly captures the nostalgic essence of an era gone by, offering a cozy haven where history and coffee converge.

A Portal to the Past:
Komiteti Café's décor and ambiance evoke the spirit of bygone days. The vintage furnishings, retro décor, and carefully curated memorabilia transport you to a time

when life had a slower pace and simpler pleasures were savored.

Timeless Atmosphere:
The café's interior is imbued with a sense of timelessness that encourages you to unwind and embrace the present moment. From the soft lighting to the soothing background music, every detail is crafted to create an atmosphere of comfort and relaxation.

Historical Nods:
The name "Komiteti" itself is a nod to Albania's past, referencing the "Komiteti i Qytetit" (City Committee) that played a role in the city's governance during the communist era. The café pays homage to this history, creating an environment that's both nostalgic and thought-provoking.

Coffee and Conversations:
As you savor a cup of coffee in Komiteti Café, you'll be transported to an era when coffeehouses were centers of intellectual exchange and meaningful conversations. Whether you're enjoying a book, engaging in friendly banter, or simply taking in the ambiance, the café invites you to connect with others in a cozy setting.

Taste of Tradition:
In addition to its nostalgic charm, Komiteti Café offers a selection of traditional Albanian pastries, sweets, and beverages that provide a taste of the country's culinary

heritage. It's a perfect opportunity to savor authentic flavors while enveloped in the café's vintage charm.

Cultural Fusion:
While embracing the past, Komiteti Café also bridges the gap between generations and cultures. It's a place where the stories of the past are shared and celebrated, fostering connections between locals and visitors who gather to experience the café's unique allure.

An Escape from Modernity:
Komiteti Café is a haven for those seeking respite from the fast-paced modern world. It's a retreat where you can detach from screens, slow down, and relish in the simple pleasures of a well-brewed coffee and genuine conversation.

A Journey Through Time:
Visiting Komiteti Café isn't just about enjoying a cup of coffee; it's about embarking on a journey through time. It's a testament to Tirana's ability to preserve its cultural heritage while embracing the present, and a reminder that the past is an ever-present source of inspiration.

A Glimpse of Yesterday:
Komiteti Café invites you to step into a different era, if only for a little while. It's a place where you can sip your coffee, bask in the atmosphere, and find comfort in the echoes of yesterday that still resonate today.

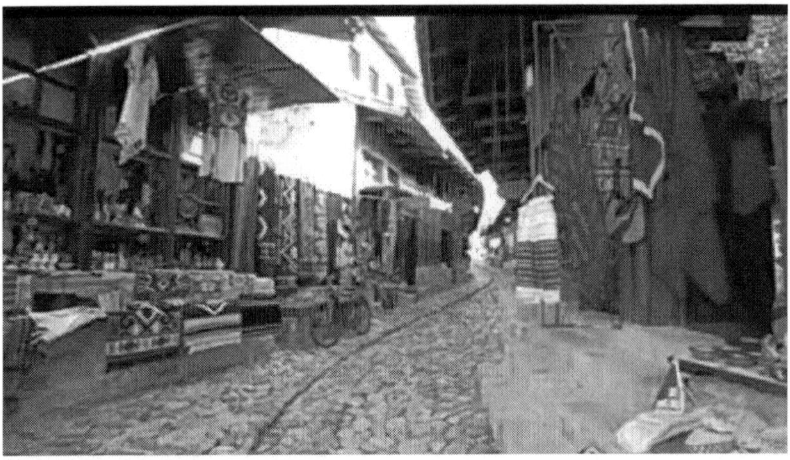

Chapter 4

Essential Sights and Landmarks

- Et'hem Bey Mosque: Architectural Marvel

Amidst the urban landscape of Tirana, a masterpiece of architectural splendor stands as a testament to the city's rich cultural heritage – the Et'hem Bey Mosque. This elegant mosque, adorned with intricate details and a storied history, represents not only a place of worship but also an artistic and cultural gem that continues to captivate visitors.

Historical Footprints:
The Et'hem Bey Mosque traces its origins back to the late 18th century, when it was commissioned by Et'hem Bey, a prominent figure in Tirana's history. Despite the country's historical shifts and changes, the mosque has stood as a silent witness to Albania's journey through time.

Architectural Intricacies:
One cannot help but be awed by the mosque's intricate architectural features. The exterior façade boasts delicate frescoes and intricate floral motifs that reflect Ottoman and Islamic design influences. The mosque's graceful minaret and dome serve as timeless symbols of spiritual reverence.

Spiritual Sanctuary:
Beyond its aesthetic beauty, the Et'hem Bey Mosque is a place of spiritual significance for Tirana's Muslim community. The interior, with its simple yet elegant design, exudes an air of tranquility that invites reflection and prayer. The mosque's courtyard provides a serene space for communal gatherings and moments of contemplation.

Message of Tolerance:
The mosque's history is woven into Albania's unique fabric of religious tolerance. Despite the challenges that history presented, the Et'hem Bey Mosque remained open and operational, a testament to the country's embrace of diversity and coexistence.

The Resilience of Art:
The Et'hem Bey Mosque also embodies the resilience of art in the face of adversity. During Albania's communist era, religious practices were restricted, and many places of worship faced challenges. The mosque's frescoes

were hidden under layers of paint to protect them, only to be unveiled once again after the fall of communism.

Cultural Gem:
Visiting the Et'hem Bey Mosque isn't just an encounter with history; it's an immersion into the rich cultural mosaic of Tirana. The mosque's significance extends beyond religious boundaries, inviting visitors to appreciate the blend of architectural influences that have shaped the city's character.

A Captivating Presence:
The Et'hem Bey Mosque stands as a captivating presence within Tirana's urban landscape. It's a destination that beckons not only to those seeking spiritual solace but also to enthusiasts of art and history who wish to explore its visual marvels.

Unity in Diversity:
In a world often divided by differences, the Et'hem Bey Mosque serves as a poignant reminder of Albania's commitment to unity in diversity. It's a living testament to the country's ethos of religious harmony and its dedication to preserving its cultural heritage.

A Treasure of Tirana:
The Et'hem Bey Mosque is more than just an architectural marvel; it's a treasure that encapsulates the spirit of Tirana itself. With every intricate detail, every historical layer, and every prayer that has echoed within

its walls, the mosque weaves a narrative that enriches the city's cultural tapestry.

- National History Museum: Stories of the Past

Immerse yourself in the rich tapestry of Albania's history at the National History Museum, a repository of stories that span centuries and offer insights into the nation's journey through time. Located in the heart of Tirana, this museum is a captivating window into Albania's past, where artifacts, exhibits, and narratives come together to weave a comprehensive tale.

Time Travel Through Exhibits:
The National History Museum invites you to embark on a time-traveling adventure. Its exhibits are meticulously curated to take you on a chronological journey, from ancient civilizations to modern times. Each hall is a chapter in Albania's history, revealing the cultural, political, and societal dynamics that have shaped the nation.

Archaeological Treasures:
Step back thousands of years as you encounter artifacts that tell the stories of Albania's earliest inhabitants. From ancient pottery to intricate jewelry, these relics offer glimpses into the daily lives, traditions, and beliefs of ancient civilizations that once thrived on Albanian soil.

Medieval Marvels:
The museum's exhibits also delve into the medieval era, showcasing the artistry and architecture that flourished during this period. Intricately carved religious icons, illuminated manuscripts, and architectural models provide a glimpse into Albania's spiritual and artistic heritage.

Ottoman and Modern Times:
As you progress through the museum's halls, you'll encounter the influence of the Ottoman Empire, a significant chapter in Albania's history. The displays shed light on the country's struggle for independence and its subsequent efforts to build a modern nation-state.

Voices of Change:
The National History Museum is not just about objects; it's about voices and narratives. Personal stories of individuals who played pivotal roles in Albania's history are woven into the exhibits, offering a human perspective that adds depth to the historical accounts.

A Journey of Identity:
The museum's role in shaping Albania's national identity is palpable. It reflects the nation's journey through triumphs and challenges, resilience and transformation, offering visitors a deeper understanding of the country's essence.

Educational Insight:
The National History Museum isn't only for historians; it's a valuable educational resource for everyone. Students, scholars, and curious minds alike can delve into the exhibits, gaining insights into the forces that have shaped Albania's past and continue to influence its present.

Reflection and Connection:
Visiting the National History Museum is more than just exploring artifacts; it's an opportunity to reflect on the threads that connect the past to the present. It's a reminder that the narratives within its walls are part of a larger global story, emphasizing the interconnectedness of human history.

A Living Chronicle:
The National History Museum stands as a living chronicle of Albania's resilience, diversity, and evolution. With every step you take within its halls, you're walking through the corridors of time, connecting with the struggles, triumphs, and aspirations of a nation that has left its mark on history.

- Pyramid of Tirana: Controversial Icon

Dominating the urban landscape of Tirana, the Pyramid stands as an enigmatic and divisive monument that embodies a complex blend of history, architecture, and controversy. Once a symbol of modernity and ambition, it has evolved into a canvas of collective memory, reflecting the city's evolution and the multifaceted perspectives of its inhabitants.

Architectural Ambition:
The Pyramid of Tirana was built in 1988 as a museum and mausoleum dedicated to Albania's former leader, Enver Hoxha. Its sleek, geometric design was meant to symbolize progress and forward-thinking, embodying an era of grand architectural ambitions.

Shifting Meanings:
Over the years, the Pyramid's purpose and symbolism shifted dramatically. It transformed from a homage to a leader into a backdrop for political and social shifts within Albania. Its identity mirrors the nation's journey from a time of isolation to a period of reimagining itself within a global context.

Cultural Canvas:
The Pyramid's exterior walls have become a canvas for graffiti, street art, and public expressions of dissent, creativity, and protest. This visual evolution captures the voices of generations, as they leave their marks on the monument, each layer contributing to its ever-changing narrative.

Collective Memory:
The Pyramid is not only a physical structure; it's also a vessel of collective memory. For older generations, it holds traces of history and a connection to the past. For

younger generations, it's a platform for dialogue, a place to discuss the nation's identity, and an architectural canvas that reflects their aspirations.

Controversial Evolution:
The Pyramid's evolving identity has sparked debates about its preservation, transformation, or removal. While some view it as a historical artifact that deserves recognition, others see it as a reminder of a repressive past. The ongoing debate encapsulates the complexity of acknowledging history while paving the way for progress.

Cultural Context:
The Pyramid's presence is a reflection of the city's layers of history and the complexities of reconciling the past with the present. It encourages contemplation about how cities evolve, how architecture becomes entwined with societal narratives, and how the built environment shapes cultural conversations.

Architectural Archaeology:
As the Pyramid ages, its weathered facade carries the marks of time – cracks, graffiti, and layers of paint. These signs of decay and change become an archaeology of architecture, telling the story of how a structure interacts with its environment and the people who inhabit it.

Aesthetic Intrigue:

Despite its controversial status, the Pyramid retains an intriguing aesthetic allure. Its form challenges traditional architectural norms, its proportions evoke curiosity, and its angular lines create a dynamic visual contrast against the cityscape.

Unending Dialogue:
The Pyramid of Tirana remains an ongoing dialogue, a testament to how architecture can transcend its original purpose and morph into a vessel for complex discussions about history, culture, and societal change. It's a reminder that even as cities evolve, the stories they tell through their structures continue to resonate with the present and shape the future.

- Dajti Mountain: Panoramic Views

Rising majestically on the outskirts of Tirana, Dajti Mountain offers a breathtaking escape into nature's embrace and a panoramic spectacle that stretches beyond the city's horizon. This natural haven beckons adventurers and nature enthusiasts to ascend its slopes, where awe-inspiring vistas, lush landscapes, and a sense of tranquility await.

A Natural Retreat:
Dajti Mountain is a sanctuary for those seeking respite from the urban pace. Just a short distance from Tirana, it transports you from the bustling cityscape to a realm of serene forests, fresh air, and the rustling of leaves – a

reminder that tranquility can be found just beyond the city's borders.

Spectacular Ascent:
The journey to Dajti's summit is an adventure in itself. A cable car ride or a scenic drive through winding roads takes you higher and higher, offering glimpses of Tirana below and gradually revealing the expansive beauty that awaits atop the mountain.

Panoramic Vistas:
Reaching Dajti's peak rewards you with panoramic vistas that defy description. From this elevated vantage point, you can witness the city's tapestry unfurl before you, framed by rolling hills, valleys, and the distant horizon. The interplay of light and shadow paints an ever-changing canvas of beauty.

Hiking Trails and Exploration:
For the adventurous at heart, Dajti offers hiking trails that meander through its forests, revealing hidden waterfalls, diverse flora, and the occasional glimpse of wildlife. The trails cater to hikers of various levels, providing an opportunity to connect with nature and disconnect from the outside world.

Mountain Escapades:
Dajti isn't just for nature enthusiasts; it's also a hub of outdoor activities. Mountain biking, paragliding, and

horseback riding are among the options that cater to those seeking an adrenaline rush amidst the pristine natural setting.

Restaurants with a View:
Atop Dajti, you'll find restaurants and cafes where you can savor local cuisine while enjoying unobstructed views. Whether you're indulging in traditional dishes or simply sipping a cup of coffee, the backdrop of endless horizons adds a touch of magic to every bite.

Sunset Magic:
As the day draws to a close, Dajti's summit becomes a prime location to witness a mesmerizing sunset. The sun's golden hues reflecting off the landscape create a scene of tranquility and beauty that lingers in memory long after the day has passed.

Connecting with Nature:
Dajti Mountain isn't just a physical destination; it's a place of rejuvenation and connection. It's a reminder of the inherent beauty of the natural world and the restorative power of spending time in its embrace.

A Tapestry of Wonder:
Visiting Dajti Mountain is a journey that transcends sightseeing; it's an opportunity to immerse yourself in the grandeur of nature's masterpiece. Whether you're standing in awe at the panoramic views or exploring the

trails that wind through its forests, Dajti offers a glimpse of a world that's both timeless and ever-changing.

- Clock Tower: Ascend Through Time

Tirana's Clock Tower stands as a silent sentinel that not only marks the passing hours but also invites you to ascend through the layers of the city's history. This iconic structure, with its unique blend of architectural styles, offers a glimpse into the city's past while granting panoramic views that stretch across its vibrant present.

A Historical Landmark:
The Clock Tower, built in the 1820s, is a living testament to Tirana's enduring history. Its elegant design reflects a fusion of Ottoman and Western architectural influences, embodying the city's historical connections with both worlds.

Architectural Harmony:
The tower's minaret-like form, adorned with decorative motifs and intricate details, speaks to the interplay of cultures that have shaped Tirana over the centuries. Its design resonates with the city's ability to harmoniously merge diverse influences into a cohesive whole.

Stepping into the Past:
Ascending the Clock Tower's narrow staircase is like stepping back in time. The journey through its interior, with its well-worn steps and ancient walls, carries you through generations of people who once climbed the same path, each with their own stories to tell.

Panoramic Perspectives:
Reaching the top of the Clock Tower rewards you with an awe-inspiring panorama that captures the essence of Tirana. The cityscape unfolds before you, revealing its bustling streets, colorful buildings, and the picturesque mountains that encircle the horizon.

Capturing the Present:
From the tower's vantage point, you'll witness Tirana's dynamic energy as it thrives in the present moment. The contrast between historic landmarks and modern developments highlights the city's evolution while offering a visual feast that spans across time.

Symbolic Passage:
The Clock Tower's ascent becomes a symbolic passage through the city's history and transformation. As you climb, you're not only traversing physical steps but also traveling through layers of culture, architecture, and the stories of the people who have called Tirana home.

Moments Frozen in Time:

At the top of the tower, you're granted a brief moment where time stands still. Amidst the brisk breeze and panoramic views, you're suspended between past and present, absorbing the beauty of the city while contemplating the threads that connect its history.

A Testament to Continuity:
The Clock Tower's enduring presence is a testament to the continuity of Tirana's identity. It reminds us that while the city evolves and modernizes, it retains a deep-rooted connection to its history, preserving its cultural heritage for generations to come.

Timeless Encounter:
Visiting the Clock Tower isn't just a climb; it's an encounter with the soul of Tirana. It's an opportunity to trace the city's narrative from its earliest days to the vibrant present, all while gazing out over its ever-changing landscape and embracing the profound connection between time and place.

Chapter 5

Embracing Tirana's Culinary Scene

- Albanian Gastronomy: An Overview

Albanian gastronomy is a vibrant tapestry woven from a rich blend of historical influences, cultural diversity, and a deep connection to the land and sea. From hearty traditional dishes to the exploration of local ingredients, Albanian cuisine offers a culinary journey that reflects the nation's identity and the flavors of its past and present.

Historical Fusion:
Albania's gastronomy bears the imprints of its diverse history. Ottoman, Mediterranean, and Balkan influences have contributed to a unique fusion of flavors, creating a cuisine that's both familiar and distinct. From kebabs to pastries, each dish carries traces of the nation's past interactions.

Farm-to-Table Philosophy:
Albanian cuisine is deeply rooted in the country's agrarian heritage. With fertile lands, abundant orchards, and coastal waters, the "farm-to-table" philosophy is ingrained in daily life. Freshness is key, and seasonal produce, herbs, and olive oil take center stage.

Traditional Staples:
Albanian cuisine boasts a repertoire of traditional dishes that resonate with both locals and visitors. Fërgesë, a comforting dish of peppers, tomatoes, and cheese, and Byrek, a savory pastry filled with various ingredients, are just a glimpse of the array of flavors waiting to be savored.

Coastal Delights:
The coastline gifts Albanian cuisine with an array of seafood delicacies. Grilled fish, octopus, and mussels take on local twists that reflect the region's coastal culture. These dishes pay homage to the sea's bounty while celebrating the art of simplicity.

Meat and Grill Culture:
Meat holds a special place in Albanian culinary tradition. Grilled meats, often marinated with aromatic herbs, are a staple at gatherings and celebrations. Lamb, pork, and beef showcase the skillful balance between tradition and innovation.

Diverse Regional Nuances:
Albania's diverse landscapes and microclimates result in a range of regional cuisines. The mountainous north offers heartier fare, while the coastal south presents dishes with a Mediterranean flair. Exploring different regions offers a deeper understanding of the country's gastronomic diversity.

Influence of Dairy:
Dairy products play a pivotal role in Albanian cuisine. Cheese, yogurt, and butter find their way into various dishes, adding a creamy richness that enhances both traditional recipes and modern interpretations.

Culinary Celebrations:
Albanian gastronomy is often celebrated during festive occasions. Wedding feasts, holidays, and gatherings are marked by abundant tables laden with dishes that symbolize abundance, hospitality, and the joy of sharing.

Cultural Heritage:
Albanian gastronomy isn't merely about food; it's a reflection of cultural heritage. The act of preparing and sharing meals brings families and communities together, preserving traditions and fostering connections that span generations.

Evolution and Innovation:
While rooted in tradition, Albanian gastronomy is also experiencing a renaissance. Chefs and food enthusiasts are exploring new interpretations of classic dishes,

incorporating contemporary techniques and international influences.

A Culinary Voyage:
Exploring Albanian gastronomy is more than just tasting dishes; it's a voyage that uncovers the layers of history, geography, and culture that contribute to the nation's unique flavors. Whether savoring time-honored recipes or indulging in modern creations, Albanian cuisine offers a tantalizing journey that delights the palate and nourishes the soul.

-Top Traditional Dishes to Try

Byrek:
Among the beloved traditional dishes of Albania, "Byrek" takes the lead. This delectable treat consists of layers of dough filled with a variety of flavorful ingredients in between. Each "Byrek" boasts its own distinctive fillings, resulting in a myriad of recipes and tastes. Popular options include "Byrek me Gjizë" (Byrek with Ricotta Cheese), "Byrek me Domate dhe Qepë" (Byrek with Onions and Tomatoes), "Byrek me Spinaq" (Byrek with Spinach), and "Byrek me Mish" (Byrek with Meat).

Tava e Kosit:
Originating from Elbasan near Tirana, "Tava e Kosit" is an authentic Albanian dish that has become a culinary staple across the country. Variations exist, but the main components include lamb meat, eggs, and yogurt.

Combined with fragrant herbs, these ingredients come together in a casserole and are oven-cooked to perfection.

Bakllava:

Indulge in the delightful dessert known as "Bakllava," a must-try in Albanian gastronomy. Although of Turkish origin, Albanians have embraced and adapted this treat over the centuries. This mouthwatering cake is composed of layers of dough filled with nuts and sugar. Often, a sweet syrup called "shërbet" is generously drizzled on top. Various bakeries add their personal touch, resulting in diverse variations of Baklava, with unique processes, ingredients, and sizes.

Speca të Mbushura:

"Speca të mbushura," or stuffed peppers, is another authentic Albanian delight, particularly favored during the summer season. These peppers are filled with a mixture of ground beef, onions, herbs, and tomato sauce, offering a tantalizing blend of flavors. The specific stuffing can vary based on the region and cook, resulting in delightful regional nuances.

Fërgesa:

Hailing from central Albania, "Fërgesa" is a native dish that can easily be savored in cities like Tirana. This flavorful meal comprises peppers, tomatoes, onions, cottage cheese, and a medley of spices. After cooking, it transforms into a thick and hearty dip, traditionally served in heat-resistant pots. "Fërgesa" embodies simplicity and taste – perfect when accompanied by bread for an authentic Albanian experience.

Qofte:
"Qofte," beloved across Albania and commonly found in local taverns, features spiced meatballs often served with a side salad. A regional variation of this dish is "Kernacka," a distinctive meatball from the Korça plain. These traditional morsels complement beverages like beer and are a favorite among locals.

Shëndetli:
Indulge in the delicious Albanian delicacy known as "Shëndetli." This dessert combines the textures of biscuits and cake, beginning as a cookie-like baked dough and evolving into a sweet and satisfying treat. Honey, nuts, eggs, and sugar form the foundation of "Shëndetli," resulting in a delightful balance of flavors and textures.

Petulla:
"Petulla," Albania's own take on doughnuts and pancakes, is a staple in the country's authentic cuisine. These fried dough bites come in fist-sized pieces and can be enjoyed with cheese for savory satisfaction or drizzled with honey for a sweet twist.

Tave Peshku (Fish in the Oven):
Along the stunning Albanian Riviera, fresh fish and seafood abound, making "Tave Peshku" a coastal delight. With simplicity as the hallmark of Albanian fish

recipes, oven-cooked fish showcases the Mediterranean's culinary finesse and freshness, offering a true taste of the sea.

Imam Bajalldi:
"Imam Bajalldi," another dish with Turkish origins, has found its place in Albanian cuisine. Reflecting centuries of Ottoman influence, this summer specialty features large stuffed eggplants baked to perfection. Variations abound, but ingredients like garlic, tomato puree, onions, and parsley often take center stage in this delicious creation.

Exploring the Delights of Traditional Albanian Cuisine

Before we embark on our culinary journey, let's delve into the world of Albanian cuisine and its intriguing offerings.

A Tapestry of Flavors and Aromas:
Albanian cuisine is renowned for its diverse palette of flavors, rich spices, and enticing aromas. The heart of the country's culinary artistry lies in its central regions, where dishes from the mountainous landscapes take center stage. From the hearty fërgesë to the savory byrek, the comforting grosh, and the enticing tavë kosi, Albanian cuisine offers a harmonious blend of tradition and taste.

Tirana's Gastronomic Treasures:
In the bustling capital city of Tirana, you'll find an array of establishments that specialize in these culinary treasures, allowing you to immerse yourself in the essence of Albanian culture and history.

1. Oda:
Nestled in the heart of Tirana, Oda presents a contemporary twist on traditional Albanian fare. With a warm ambiance and impeccable service, this modern eatery offers not only delectable main courses but also a tantalizing selection of traditional desserts and homemade ice cream. Located on Luigj Gurakuqi Street, Oda provides an inviting space for friends to gather, unwind, and savor the culinary delights of the region.

2. Era:
Era, a family-operated gem in Tirana, boasts a blend of local and international flavors. A commitment to fresh, organic ingredients shines through in their innovative take on traditional recipes. Situated near the Air Albania Stadium, Era welcomes guests with an inviting atmosphere and a menu that pays homage to Albanian culinary heritage while embracing modern culinary techniques.

3. Kapelet:
Kapelet, a unique establishment adorned with an unconventional ceiling decoration of hats, offers a delightful journey into traditional Albanian cuisine.

Perched on a small hill, this restaurant rewards visitors with a panoramic view of Tirana. A menu featuring a diverse range of meat dishes, seafood, and salads crafted from fresh ingredients awaits patrons, making the journey to Shkoze, where Kapelet resides, a rewarding culinary adventure.

4. Mullixhiu:
Stepping into Mullixhiu is like stepping into a rustic haven of warmth and hospitality. This beloved restaurant caters to both locals and tourists, serving dishes prepared with organic, nourishing ingredients. Amidst its cozy ambiance, guests can relish a selection of wines, beers, and Albanian specialties such as qofte me mish (meatballs), tave kosi (yogurt casserole), and byrek. Mullixhiu's location near the serene Artificial Lake Park provides a natural backdrop that complements its commitment to wholesome dining.

5. Mrizi i Zanave:
Affectionately known as "The Vineyard of Dreams," Mrizi i Zanave stands as an iconic Tirana restaurant. Offering traditional Albanian cuisine within the walls of a stunning 19th-century mansion, this establishment provides not only culinary delights but also breathtaking views of the cityscape. From its perch in the old district of the city, Mrizi i Zanave offers an intimate setting to savor romantic dinners and drinks while relishing the city's panorama. Impeccable service and artful presentation transform each plate into an irresistible masterpiece.

As we venture forth into the world of Albanian cuisine, these establishments beckon with their unique interpretations of traditional dishes, inviting you to savor the cultural tapestry woven through every bite.

- Best Local Eateries and Restaurants

Tirana stands as a haven for exceptional dining, boasting a collection of upscale restaurants nestled within the city center. These establishments curate a refined atmosphere that revolves around the pillars of quality cuisine, impeccable service, and a captivating ambiance. These fine dining venues transcend mere nourishment, focusing on the artistry of the dining experience itself. The emphasis isn't on quantity, but rather the intricate interplay of flavors, textures, and aesthetics that create an unforgettable memory.

Explore our Selection of Fine Dining Establishments:

1. Salt:
Situated in the iconic Blloku area, a vibrant hub in Tirana known for its culinary delights, Salt takes you on a Mediterranean gastronomic journey. Exquisite seafood and sushi are just a glimpse of their offerings. With a captivating setting and tasteful decor, Salt ensures you'll revel in the complete fine dining experience. Find Salt at Pjeter Bogdani Street.

2. Á la Santè:

A la Sante specializes in the elegance of French cuisine. Classic dishes such as steak tartare, escargot, and foie gras grace their menu. The inviting ambiance, complete with a spacious outdoor patio and a wood-fired oven, makes for a delightful setting to savor dishes prepared with locally-sourced ingredients. Discover Á la Santè at Sami Frasheri Street.

3. Padam:

Nestled in the heart of Tirana, Padam elevates Albanian cuisine with a modern twist. The restaurant's elegant interior complements a diverse menu that promises to linger in your memory. With its location on Papa Gjon Pali II Street, Padam beckons you to savor inventive culinary creations.

4. Kripë dhe Piper:

The essence of taste is celebrated at Kripë dhe Piper, aptly named for salt and pepper in Albanian. Authenticity takes center stage here, with a menu that tantalizes the palate with intriguing dishes. Friendly and attentive staff contribute to an exceptional dining experience at this Sami Frasheri Street gem.

5. Estia:

Vila Estia, nestled in one of Tirana's oldest neighborhoods, exudes tranquility and elegance. Housed in a captivating 1940s villa boasting Italian-style architecture and modern touches, Estia offers an enchanting backdrop for your dining aspirations. This is where culinary artistry harmonizes with the melodies of classical music, ideal for romantic dinners and cherished family gatherings.

Elevate your culinary journey in Tirana by embracing the refined offerings of these fine dining establishments. Each venue weaves a tale of flavors, ambience, and attentive service, inviting you to indulge in the art of dining.

-Savoring Budget-Friendly Delights: Where to Enjoy Delectable Eats

Discovering delectable yet affordable dining options in Tirana is a delightful adventure. From local street food vendors to well-known fast-food chains, the city offers a plethora of choices that won't strain your wallet. Whether you're seeking a culinary journey on a budget or simply looking to indulge in flavors without breaking the bank, Tirana's array of cheap eats beckons.

1. Grano Tenero:
Nestled in the Pazari i Ri area, Grano Tenero invites you to savor an array of unique pizzas adorned with creative toppings. Its unassuming yet inviting decor, characterized by wood furnishings and expansive glass windows, sets the stage for a delightful dining experience. For added charm, dine in the cozy outdoor

area adorned with wooden decorations. Discover Grano Tenero's culinary delights at Tefta Tashko-Koco Street.

2. Pizzarte Tirana:
Founded by two Italian chefs in 2014, Pizzarte Tirana has captured hearts with its authentic Italian pizzas. Crafted from fresh ingredients and handmade dough, these pizzas are expertly cooked in a traditional Italian oven, infusing them with a distinct smoky flavor. Immerse yourself in genuine Italian pizza at Pizzarte, conveniently located on Luigj Gurakuqi Street.

3. Ópa:
A popular fast-food chain dotting the landscape of Tirana, Ópa introduces a taste of Greek street food to the city. From gyros to burgers and loukoumades, each offering carries its own unique charm and flavor. The bustling Blloku area hosts one of the most beloved Ópa locations, adorned with vibrant decor and a vibrant ambiance.

4. Capitol:
A favored destination for the city's youth, Capitol stands as one of Tirana's top fast-food spots. Its expansive menu features an array of mouthwatering burgers, pizzas, sandwiches, and more. Known for affordability, quality fare, and friendly service, Capitol provides a haven for flavor enthusiasts. Pay a visit to Capitol on Kavaja Street, open every day until midnight.

5. Kok' a Pulë:
Kok a Pulë satisfies cravings for classic favorites like burgers, hot dogs, and cheddar fries. With generous portions, wallet-friendly prices, and a welcoming atmosphere, it's a sought-after choice for a late-night rendezvous with friends. Its 24-hour operation ensures you're never far from satisfying your hunger. Experience the warmth and flavor of Kok a Pulë on Mine Peza Street.

As you traverse the culinary landscape of Tirana, let these options guide you to memorable dining experiences that offer a perfect balance of flavor and affordability.

-International Cuisine in Tirana

Top International Eateries in Tirana

1. Yamato:
For an exceptional sushi experience, look no further than Yamato. This esteemed establishment not only boasts an array of sushi creations but also offers a range of traditional Japanese dishes such as tempura, teriyaki, and bento boxes. The modern and chic ambiance creates an international dining atmosphere. A sushi bar allows you to witness the culinary artistry firsthand. Find Yamato conveniently close to Tirana's

city center on Papa Gjon Pali Street – a true taste of Japanese culture awaits.

2. Serendiville & Serendipity the Mexican:
Yearning for authentic Mexican flavors? Serendipity beckons you into an atmosphere brimming with vibrancy and warmth. From tacos and burritos to nachos and quesadillas, a plethora of Mexican delights awaits your palate. With two locations – Skender Luarasi Street and Ibrahim Rugova Street – Serendipity ensures an unforgettable Mexican journey, no matter where you choose to indulge.

3. Chakra Indian Fusion:
Nestled in Tirana's center, Chakra Indian Fusion marries Indian and European cuisines with modern flair. Savor the essence of traditional Indian dishes, from curries to tandoori, alongside an array of European fare. The restaurant's lively atmosphere resonates with both locals and visitors, offering a symphony of flavors and vibrant vibes. Discover Chakra's fusion brilliance next to Kinema Millenium on Murat Toptani Street.

4. Amazonic Tirana:
Step into Amazonic's contemporary world, nestled within the Arena Center. The restaurant's captivating jungle-themed decor, adorned with animals and greenery, sets the stage for a unique culinary experience. Offering a diverse international menu – spanning Italian, Mexican, and Indian cuisines – Amazonic ensures each dish is a masterpiece of flavor.

Seek out Amazonic near Tirana Stadium, within Arena Center, Entrance BC.

5. Metropolitan Restaurant:
The Metropolitan Restaurant is a culinary gem offering a global gastronomic adventure. From international delicacies to traditional Albanian fare, the menu caters to diverse palates. The elegant interior, bathed in sunlight through expansive glass windows, creates an inviting ambiance. For those seeking al fresco dining, a spacious terrace awaits. Find Metropolitan within Albania Hotel, located at Italia Square – a culinary journey that knows no borders.

- Tirana's Coffee Culture

Tirana's coffee culture is a vibrant and integral part of daily life, shaping social interactions, work routines, and leisurely moments. The city's streets are adorned with a plethora of cafes, each offering a unique experience that embodies the spirit of Albanian hospitality and the love for rich, aromatic brews.

A Ritual of Connection:
Coffee in Tirana is not merely a beverage but a ritual that fosters connections and conversations. The act of sharing a cup of coffee transcends the functional, symbolizing a pause from the hustle and bustle of life to savor the present moment. Whether it's catching up with friends, discussing business matters, or simply

people-watching, coffee forms the backdrop of these interactions.

Diverse Coffee Offerings:
Tirana's coffee culture embraces a variety of coffee preparations, each with its own distinct charm. From the strong and short espresso to the velvety texture of cappuccinos and lattes, cafes cater to different preferences. The traditional Turkish-style coffee, known as "kafe turke," also holds its place, offering a taste of heritage and tradition.

Cafes as Gathering Spaces:
Cafes in Tirana are more than just places to grab a drink; they serve as communal hubs where locals and visitors alike come together. Whether it's a small local cafe with a charming atmosphere or a modern establishment with trendy decor, each cafe offers a unique ambiance. Patrons often linger, engaging in animated discussions or quietly working on laptops while sipping their favorite brew.

Boulevard of Cafes:
Tirana's central boulevards, such as the bustling "Dëshmorët e Kombit" Boulevard and the trendy "Ibrahim Rugova" Street, are lined with cafes that spill out onto the sidewalks. These cafes create a dynamic and inviting atmosphere, inviting passersby to pause and enjoy a cup of coffee while observing the city's pulse.

A Blend of Tradition and Modernity:
While Tirana's coffee culture embraces tradition and the art of slow enjoyment, it also welcomes modern trends. Specialty coffee shops have emerged, catering to coffee enthusiasts seeking carefully sourced beans and intricate brewing methods. This fusion of old and new adds depth to the city's coffee landscape.

Beyond the Brew:
Tirana's coffee culture extends beyond the beverage itself. Many cafes offer an array of pastries, desserts, and light bites that perfectly complement the coffee experience. From traditional sweet treats to contemporary delights, these accompaniments enhance the overall sensory journey.

Embrace the Ritual:
To truly immerse yourself in Tirana's coffee culture, take the time to visit a local cafe, order your preferred brew, and allow yourself to savor not just the coffee but the connections, conversations, and atmosphere that come with it. Whether you're a visitor or a resident, Tirana's cafes offer a window into the heart of the city's social fabric, inviting you to partake in a time-honored tradition that continues to evolve with each cup poured.

- Sweet Delights: Desserts and Pastries

Tirana's culinary landscape is not only rich in savory dishes but also boasts a tantalizing array of desserts and pastries that cater to every sweet tooth. From traditional Albanian treats to international confections, the city offers a delectable journey through sugary delights.

1. Baklava: A time-honored treat that has traveled from Turkey to Albania, baklava is a delicate pastry made with layers of thin filo dough, nuts, and sweet syrup. It's a symphony of textures and flavors that embodies the essence of Albanian sweets.

2. Tavë Kosi: While not your typical dessert, this Albanian custard dish made from yogurt, eggs, and rice is a unique and delightful way to end a meal. It's often flavored with herbs and spices, creating a savory-sweet balance that's truly special.

3. Krofne: These fluffy doughnuts, known as krofne, are popular street treats. They're often dusted with powdered sugar and sometimes filled with jams or creams, making them a delightful on-the-go snack.

4. Trilece: A moist and creamy dessert, trilece is akin to a milk-soaked cake that melts in your mouth. Topped with caramel, it's a true comfort indulgence that's adored by locals.

5. Shendetli: Combining the best of both biscuit and cake textures, shendetli is a dessert that pairs the crunch of biscuits with the sweetness of cake. Nuts, honey, eggs, and sugar are the key ingredients that create this delightful treat.

6. Bakllava: A testament to the cultural fusion in Tirana, bakllava is an Albanian take on the classic Middle Eastern pastry. Layers of filo dough, nuts, and sweet syrup create a harmonious blend of flavors and textures.

7. Mëllëfik: This traditional Albanian dessert is a masterpiece of pastry artistry. Made with thin layers of dough and a sweet filling, it's often adorned with intricate designs and patterns.

8. Crepes: Whether filled with chocolate, fruit, or a combination of flavors, crepes are a beloved street food that caters to every palate. They're a versatile and delicious treat that can be enjoyed any time of day.

9. Pallaqinka: Similar to crepes, pallaqinka are thin pancakes that are rolled up with a variety of fillings, from jam to Nutella, creating a delightful hand-held dessert.

10. Sufllaqe: Though typically considered a savory dish, sufllaqe (skewered meat) can also be found in a sweet version. Sufllaqe e Sheqerit features chunks of sweetened meat that are grilled to perfection, providing an unexpected twist on dessert.

Whether you're strolling through local markets or visiting charming cafes, Tirana's dessert scene invites you to savor each sweet bite. From the familiar to the novel, these desserts and pastries offer a taste of both tradition and innovation, making your culinary exploration truly unforgettable.

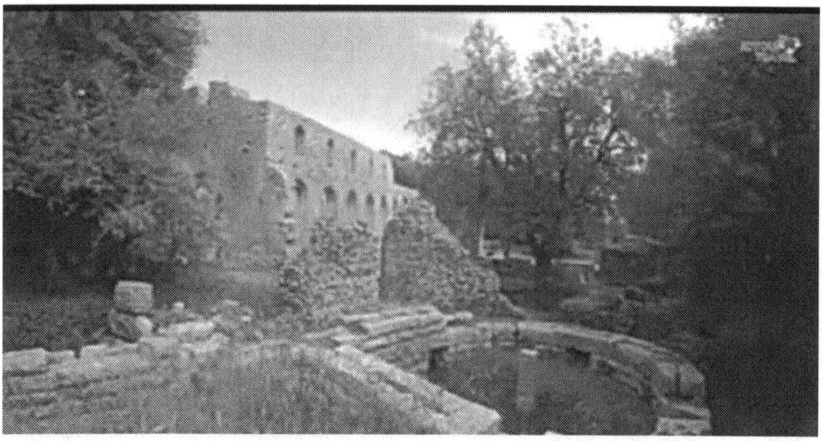

Chapter 6

Immersing in Local Experiences

- Attending Festivals and Events

Tirana's vibrant cultural scene comes alive through an exciting array of festivals and events that captivate both locals and visitors. From traditional celebrations to contemporary gatherings, these occasions offer a unique insight into the city's dynamic spirit and rich heritage.

TIFF-Tirana International Film Festival
The Tirana International Film Festival was the first international film festival in Albania, and, with the Sarajevo Film festival, it is the most famous event in the Balkans that is dedicated to cinema. Since its first edition in 2003, TIFF has aimed to reunite some of the most important filmmakers, producers, and distributors from around the world. TIFF, which usually takes place in the fall, is the only film festival in the Balkans with an official Academy Awards recognition.

TILF-Tirana International Literature Festival
During the last weekend of October, authors from Albania and other European countries are invited to dialogue with each other and the public (mostly students and literature buffs) about literature and actuality. The Tirana International Literature Festival is organized by the Institute for Democracy, Media and Culture (IDMC) and Allianz Kulturstiftung Berlin, in cooperation with the Albanian Ministry of Culture.

Nyou Festival
Nyou Festival is a music festival held in Tirana's recently renovated amphitheater, situated in the Grand Park of Tirana, near a beautiful artificial lake. The festival, which takes place every June, is dedicated to jazz music and is a great event to discover some of the best jazz artists in Albania, as well as the Balkan Peninsula.

Peza*n Fest
Peza*n Fest is one of the most important events in the country. It takes place every September in the lovely village of Peza, a hamlet located just one hour from Tirana. Peza*n Fest hosts Albanian and international artists who are happy to exhibit in a very beautiful, but very underrated place. The festival is a good occasion to discover one of the least visited areas of the country and to taste excellent traditional food prepared for the occasion.

Jazz in Albania

For music lovers, Tirana is one of the best destinations in the Balkans. The capital city of Albania is home to Jazz in Albania, a music festival dedicated to jazz music. It is hosted in Rogner Hotel, one of the most famous hotels in the country. Every July, many bands from Albania, China, Israel, USA and across Europe play their songs and entertain the international audiences in Tirana.

Albanian National Folk Festival

Immerse yourself in the country's traditional music and dance at this vibrant event. Witness vibrant costumes, intricate choreography, and lively performances that pay tribute to Albania's cultural heritage.

Tirana Beer Festival

A feast for beer connoisseurs and food lovers alike, this festival showcases craft beers and culinary delights. Attendees can savor an array of local and global brews while enjoying live music and entertainment.

International Documentary Film Festival (DocuTIFF)

Explore the world through the lens of documentaries that delve into diverse themes and stories. DocuTIFF provides a platform for thought-provoking films that shed light on global issues and human experiences.

Tirana Art Fest

The city transforms into an open-air gallery for this celebration of visual arts. Attendees can admire various art forms, from paintings and sculptures to installations and interactive exhibits.

Tirana Rock Festival
Rock music enthusiasts converge for electrifying performances by local and international bands. The festival injects the city with pulsating beats, showcasing the enduring spirit of rock and roll.

Independence Day Celebrations
Join the locals in commemorating Albania's independence with parades, concerts, and patriotic displays. The festivities capture the country's pride and unity, providing a glimpse into its historical significance.

Albanian Wine Festival
Raise your glass to Albanian winemaking traditions at this lively event. Sample a range of local wines while enjoying live music and entertainment, celebrating the country's burgeoning wine scene.

From artistic expressions to cultural traditions, Tirana's festivals and events offer a window into the city's vibrant soul. Whether you're seeking music, film, literature, or simply a lively atmosphere, these occasions invite you to immerse yourself in the heart of Tirana's cultural tapestry.

- Art and Music Scene of Tirana

Tirana's cultural heartbeat is felt through its thriving art and music scene, which resonates with creativity and expression. From contemporary galleries to live music venues, the city offers a dynamic space for both artists and enthusiasts to engage with a diverse range of artistic forms.

Contemporary Art Galleries:
Tirana boasts a burgeoning contemporary art scene, with galleries that showcase the works of both local and international artists. Explore these venues to immerse yourself in thought-provoking exhibitions, innovative installations, and a wide spectrum of artistic styles.

Music Venues and Concert Halls:
The city's musical landscape is equally vibrant, with a myriad of venues catering to various genres and tastes. From intimate jazz clubs to larger concert halls, Tirana offers a stage for local talents and international acts, ensuring that music enthusiasts have a plethora of options to choose from.

Street Art and Urban Expression:
As you wander the streets of Tirana, you'll encounter vibrant murals and graffiti that contribute to the city's urban aesthetic. Street art is an integral part of Tirana's cultural identity, showcasing both visual creativity and social commentary.

Cultural Events and Festivals:
Tirana comes alive with cultural events and festivals that celebrate the arts. From film festivals that honor cinematic achievements to music festivals that bring together diverse genres, these occasions provide platforms for artists to shine and audiences to engage.

Local Music and Dance:
Immerse yourself in the sounds of Tirana by exploring the local music and dance traditions. From traditional folk performances to modern interpretations, you can experience the rich tapestry of Albanian culture through melodies and rhythms.

Theater and Performance Arts:
Tirana's theaters and performance spaces offer a platform for dramatic arts to flourish. Attend theatrical productions, dance performances, and other live shows that showcase the city's theatrical prowess.

Cultural Workshops and Studios:
For those looking to engage actively in the creative process, Tirana offers a range of workshops and studios. Whether you're interested in painting, pottery, music, or dance, you can participate and learn from experienced artists.

Cafes and Cultural Hangouts:
Cafes and cultural hubs around Tirana often double as spaces for artistic expression. Enjoy a cup of coffee

while listening to live music, poetry readings, or engaging in conversations with fellow art enthusiasts.

Public Events and Open-Air Performances:
Tirana's parks and squares occasionally host open-air performances, from music concerts to theatrical presentations. These events allow the public to engage with the arts in a communal and accessible setting.

Artisan Markets and Craft Fairs:
Support local artists and artisans by visiting craft fairs and artisan markets. These events showcase handmade crafts, artworks, and unique creations that reflect the city's creative spirit.

Tirana's art and music scene is a vibrant tapestry that weaves together tradition, innovation, and cultural diversity. Whether you're a seasoned enthusiast or a curious explorer, you'll find ample opportunities to immerse yourself in the artistic fabric of the city.

- Shopping in Bazaars and Boutiques

Tirana's shopping experience is a captivating fusion of traditional bazaars and modern boutiques, offering a wide array of products to suit various tastes and preferences. Whether you're seeking unique souvenirs, local crafts, or high-end fashion, the city's shopping destinations promise an exciting and diverse shopping spree.

1. Bazaars and Markets:
Tirana's bazaars and markets offer a lively and authentic shopping experience. Explore the historic New Bazaar (Pazari i Ri), where you'll find a vibrant mix of stalls selling everything from fresh produce and artisanal crafts to clothing and accessories. This bustling hub is an excellent place to immerse yourself in Tirana's local culture and discover one-of-a-kind items.

2. Boutiques and Fashion:
For fashion enthusiasts, Tirana boasts a variety of boutiques that cater to diverse styles. Wander through the streets around Blloku, where you can explore an array of boutiques showcasing the latest trends in clothing, footwear, and accessories.

3. Traditional Crafts and Souvenirs:
Celebrate Tirana's heritage by exploring shops that showcase local craftsmanship. From intricately designed jewelry and handwoven textiles to ceramics and woodwork, these establishments offer an opportunity to take home a piece of Albanian culture and artistry.

4. Concept Stores and Design Shops:
Experience the contemporary side of Tirana's shopping scene by visiting concept stores and design shops. These curated spaces feature a unique blend of locally designed products, home goods, and lifestyle items that reflect the city's modern and creative spirit.

5. Antique and Vintage:
Uncover the charm of the past by exploring Tirana's antique shops and vintage boutiques. Visit the Old Bazaar (Pazari i Vjetër) to browse through an assortment of vintage treasures, where you might find unique collectibles and timeless pieces.

6. Art Galleries and Studios:
Immerse yourself in Tirana's artistic realm by visiting galleries and studios that offer artworks for sale. From paintings and sculptures to photography and crafts, these spaces allow you to bring a touch of Tirana's creativity into your own space.

7. Bookstores and Cultural Shops:
Indulge your intellectual curiosity by perusing local bookstores and cultural shops. Discover a range of Albanian literature, travel guides, and unique gifts that reflect the city's intellectual and cultural heritage.

8. Farmers' Markets:
Experience Tirana's agricultural abundance by exploring farmers' markets. Here, you can find an array of fresh produce, local delicacies, and traditional goods while engaging with local farmers and producers.

9. Souvenir Shops:
Capture the essence of your Tirana journey with charming souvenirs. Browse souvenir shops for a selection of keepsakes, from keychains and magnets to traditional crafts, offering lasting memories of your visit.

10. Shopping Malls:
For a modern shopping escapade, Tirana's shopping malls provide a comprehensive range of shops, boutiques, and international brands. These modern complexes cater to various needs, including fashion, electronics, and more.

Tirana's shopping landscape invites you to indulge in a diverse and vibrant retail adventure. Whether you're drawn to the allure of bazaars or the allure of boutiques, Tirana offers a dynamic range of shopping experiences that cater to every shopper's desires.

- Enjoying Tirana's Nightlife

When the sun sets, Tirana transforms into a vibrant hub of nightlife and entertainment, offering a diverse array of experiences that cater to every preference. From lively bars and clubs to relaxed lounges and cultural venues, Tirana's nightlife promises to keep you enthralled until the early hours of the morning.

1. Bars and Pubs:
Tirana's bar scene is bustling with energy, featuring an array of establishments that cater to various tastes. Whether you're seeking craft cocktails, local brews, or international spirits, you'll find cozy pubs and trendy bars scattered throughout the city.

2. Nightclubs and Dance Floors:

For those who love to dance the night away, Tirana's nightclubs beckon with pulsating beats and electrifying atmospheres. With a mix of genres and styles, these venues offer a chance to let loose and revel in the city's vibrant party spirit.

3. Live Music Venues:

Music enthusiasts will find their haven in Tirana's live music venues, where local bands and international acts take the stage. Whether you're into rock, jazz, electronic, or world music, these venues offer unforgettable performances that resonate through the night.

4. Rooftop Bars and Terraces:

Elevate your nightlife experience by visiting Tirana's rooftop bars and terraces. Enjoy panoramic views of the city's illuminated skyline as you savor cocktails and engage in conversations amidst a chic and stylish ambiance.

5. Cultural Events and Performances:

Tirana's cultural venues occasionally host nighttime events and performances, including theater shows, concerts, and film screenings. Immerse yourself in artistic expressions that enrich your night with creativity and emotion.

6. Late-Night Cafes and Snack Spots:
For a more relaxed yet engaging experience, Tirana offers late-night cafes and eateries that keep their doors open well into the night. Sip on coffee, savor local delicacies, and enjoy conversations with friends in a cozy atmosphere.

7. Art Galleries and Exhibitions:
Experience art in a new light by attending nighttime art exhibitions and gallery openings. These events provide an opportunity to engage with visual creativity while mingling with fellow art enthusiasts.

8. Food and Night Bazaars:
Discover Tirana's culinary delights even after sunset by visiting night bazaars and food markets. Taste local street food, sample international cuisines, and immerse yourself in a gastronomic journey under the starry sky.

9. Movie Theaters and Film Screenings:
For cinephiles, Tirana's movie theaters offer nighttime film screenings that provide an alternative way to enjoy the city's cultural offerings. Watch classic films, new releases, and indie gems in a cinematic setting.

10. Socializing and Mingling:
Tirana's nightlife is not just about the venues; it's also about the people you meet. Engage in conversations, make new friends, and connect with both locals and fellow travelers as you navigate the city's dynamic social scene.

Tirana's nightlife is a mosaic of experiences that cater to different tastes and moods. Whether you're seeking high-energy dance floors or tranquil conversations over drinks, the city's after-dark offerings ensure that your evenings are as vibrant and captivating as your days.

- Connecting with Locals: Language and Etiquette

To truly immerse yourself in the vibrant culture of Tirana, connecting with locals is key. Whether you're exploring the city's attractions or enjoying its culinary delights, understanding the local language and practicing proper etiquette can enhance your experience and foster meaningful interactions.

1. Language:
While Albanian is the official language of Tirana, many locals, especially in urban areas, also speak English, Italian, and other European languages. However, making an effort to learn a few basic phrases in Albanian can go a long way in building rapport and showing respect.

- **Greetings:** Saying "Tungjatjeta" (Good day) or "Mirëdita" (Good afternoon) is a polite way to greet locals.

- **Thank You:** Express gratitude with "Faleminderit."

- **Please:** Use "Ju lutem" when making requests.

- **Excuse Me:** Say "Më falni" to get someone's attention or apologize.

2. Etiquette:
Tirana's culture is characterized by warmth and hospitality. Observing local etiquette can help you navigate social situations and foster positive interactions.

- **Greetings:** A handshake is a common greeting, with direct eye contact and a warm smile.

- **Dress Code:** Dress modestly and respectfully, especially when visiting religious sites or formal places.

- **Personal Space:** Albanians have a warm and friendly approach to personal space, so don't be surprised by close conversations.

- **Gift Giving:** If invited to a local's home, consider bringing a small gift, like sweets or flowers, as a token of appreciation.

- **Dining Etiquette:** When dining with locals, wait for the host to initiate the meal and say "Të bëftë mirë" (Bon appétit) before eating. Engage in conversation, and don't hesitate to ask questions about the dishes.

3. Social Interactions:
Engaging in social interactions with locals can lead to meaningful cultural exchanges and new friendships.

- **Curiosity:** Ask locals about their traditions, hobbies, and favorite spots in Tirana. They'll likely be eager to share their insights.

- **Coffee Culture:** Tirana's coffee culture is a social cornerstone. Joining locals for a coffee at cafes is a great way to connect and engage in conversations.

- **Events and Festivals:** Attend local events and festivals to experience the culture firsthand and interact with locals who are proud to share their traditions.

4. Respect for Customs:
Albanians take pride in their cultural customs and traditions. Show respect by being open-minded and showing interest in their way of life.

- **Religion:** If visiting religious sites, dress modestly and observe respectful behavior, even if you're not of the same faith.

- **Traditions:** Participate in local customs and celebrations with enthusiasm, whether it's a traditional dance, a family gathering, or a holiday festival.

5. Genuine Interest:
Above all, showing genuine interest and respect for Tirana's culture and its people will lead to enriching and authentic connections.

6. Embrace Hospitality:
Albanians are known for their warm hospitality, and it's common to be invited into someone's home for a meal or a cup of coffee. If you receive such an invitation, accepting it is a wonderful opportunity to experience local life firsthand. Express your gratitude and appreciation for their hospitality, and be prepared for a generous and hearty welcome.

7. Non-Verbal Communication:
Non-verbal cues can also play a significant role in connecting with locals. A genuine smile, a nod of understanding, and maintaining eye contact during conversations all convey your interest and respect. Be attentive to the body language of your conversation partner to ensure you're communicating effectively.

8. Learning and Sharing:
Beyond language and etiquette, engaging with locals often involves a mutual exchange of knowledge and experiences. Share stories from your own culture, travels, and interests, and listen eagerly to their stories

in return. This exchange can bridge cultural gaps and foster a sense of camaraderie.

9. Participate in Community Activities:
Tirana's community events and activities provide excellent opportunities to interact with locals. Whether it's a neighborhood festival, a charity event, or a cultural workshop, participating allows you to connect on a personal level and contribute to the local community.

10. Be Open-Minded:
Approach interactions with an open mind and a genuine desire to learn. Embrace differences and appreciate the diversity of perspectives you'll encounter. Engaging in meaningful conversations about various topics, from history to daily life, can deepen your connection with locals and broaden your understanding of Tirana's culture.

11. Digital Connections:
In the age of technology, connecting with locals extends beyond face-to-face interactions. Engage with Tirana's online communities, social media groups, and forums to ask questions, seek recommendations, and connect with both locals and fellow travelers who share your interests.

12. Respect Local Norms:
Tirana is a melting pot of cultures, and understanding and respecting the norms of the city is essential. Be aware of sensitive topics, cultural taboos, and social

conventions, and navigate conversations and interactions with care and sensitivity.

Connecting with locals in Tirana is a gateway to a richer and more authentic travel experience. By embracing their language, customs, and ways of life, you'll forge genuine connections that offer insight into the heart and soul of this captivating city. Remember, every interaction is an opportunity to learn, grow, and create lasting memories.

Chapter 7

Day Trips and Excursions

- Kruja: Historical Day Trip

Just a short drive from Tirana, the ancient city of Kruja awaits, offering a captivating journey through Albania's rich history and culture. This historical day trip is a must for travelers seeking to immerse themselves in the country's past while enjoying stunning landscapes and unique attractions.

1. Departure from Tirana:
Begin your day trip by departing from Tirana in the early morning. The scenic drive to Kruja takes approximately one hour, allowing you to soak in the changing landscapes and countryside views along the way.

2. Kruja Castle:
Upon arriving in Kruja, your first stop is the iconic Kruja Castle. Perched on a hilltop, the castle provides panoramic vistas of the surrounding mountains and valleys. Explore the castle's ruins, including the medieval walls, watchtowers, and the fascinating Ethnographic Museum located within its grounds.

3. Skanderbeg Museum:
Dive into the history of Albania's national hero, Gjergj Kastrioti Skanderbeg, at the Skanderbeg Museum. This museum pays tribute to the warrior's remarkable life and his role in defending Albania against Ottoman invasions. Discover artifacts, weaponry, and historical exhibitions that shed light on Skanderbeg's legacy.

4. Old Bazaar:
Step into the heart of Kruja's past by wandering through the Old Bazaar, a bustling market filled with stalls selling local crafts, textiles, and souvenirs. Immerse yourself in the vibrant atmosphere as you interact with artisans and merchants, and perhaps pick up a unique memento to remember your journey.

5. Ethnographic Museum:
Delve into Albanian folklore and traditions at the Ethnographic Museum located within the Old Bazaar. This charming museum showcases authentic artifacts, traditional clothing, and household items, offering a glimpse into daily life during various historical periods.

6. Lunch with a View:
Enjoy a leisurely lunch at one of the local restaurants offering traditional Albanian cuisine. Savor regional dishes, such as byrek, tave kosi, and fresh salads, while relishing the picturesque views that Kruja's elevated location affords.

7. Bektashi World Center:
Visit the Bektashi World Center, a significant spiritual site for followers of the Bektashi order of Islam. Explore the complex, which includes a mosque, a tekke (spiritual gathering place), and lush gardens. Learn about the history and teachings of this mystical Sufi order while appreciating the tranquil surroundings.

8. Free Time to Explore:
After your guided visits, take some free time to explore Kruja at your own pace. Stroll through the charming streets, engage with locals, and discover hidden gems. You might want to explore local cafes, interact with artisans, or simply soak in the unique ambiance of the town.

- Durres: Sun, Sea, and History

Nestled along the picturesque Albanian coastline, Durres beckons travelers with its enticing blend of sun-soaked beaches and rich historical heritage. This coastal city is a perfect destination for those seeking a balance between leisurely seaside activities and exploring the echoes of ancient civilizations.

1. Departure from Tirana:
Embark on a scenic journey from Tirana to Durres, a relatively short drive that takes you through rolling hills and glimpses of the Adriatic Sea. The anticipation builds

as you approach the coast, eager to immerse yourself in the charms of Durres.

2. Durres Amphitheatre:
Step back in time as you visit the impressive Durres Amphitheatre, a testament to the city's Roman past. This ancient arena once hosted gladiator contests and performances, and today it stands as one of the most well-preserved amphitheatres in the Balkans. Wander through its corridors and imagine the events that unfolded within its walls centuries ago.

3. Durres Beaches:
After your historical exploration, indulge in some relaxation on Durres' pristine beaches. The city boasts a long stretch of coastline dotted with sandy shores and clear blue waters. Whether you're in the mood for sunbathing, swimming, or simply enjoying the coastal breeze, Durres' beaches offer an idyllic escape.

4. Durres Archaeological Museum:
Continue your journey through history at the Durres Archaeological Museum. This institution houses a remarkable collection of artifacts that span different epochs, from the ancient Illyrians to the Ottoman era. Marvel at the intricate jewelry, pottery, and sculptures that provide insights into the city's rich past.

5. Venetian Tower and Old City Walls:
Explore Durres' Venetian Tower, a striking stone fortress that stands as a reminder of the city's medieval history.

The tower offers panoramic views of the cityscape and the Adriatic Sea, making it a perfect vantage point for capturing memorable photos. As you walk along the Old City Walls, imagine the stories that these walls have witnessed over the centuries.

6. Seafront Promenade:
Stroll along the vibrant seafront promenade, a hub of activity and local culture. Cafes, restaurants, and shops line the waterfront, offering a taste of Durres' bustling energy. As you walk, enjoy the sea breeze and take in the sights of fishing boats and sailboats gently swaying in the harbor.

7. Lunch with a Sea View:
Savor a delicious seafood lunch at one of the waterfront restaurants, where you can indulge in fresh catches from the Adriatic Sea. As you dine, soak in the stunning views of the sea and the city's lively atmosphere.

8. Durres Byzantine Forum:
Explore the remnants of the Durres Byzantine Forum, a historical site that once served as the heart of the city's civic and economic life. Wander through the ancient ruins, imagining the forum bustling with activity during its prime.

9. Durres Ethnographic Museum:
End your exploration by delving into Albanian culture at the Durres Ethnographic Museum. Discover traditional

clothing, crafts, and household items that reflect the daily life and traditions of the region's communities.

Durres invites you to experience the perfect blend of leisure and history, where days of beachside relaxation seamlessly intertwine with explorations of ancient ruins and artifacts. Whether you're drawn to the sun, the sea, or the echoes of centuries past, Durres promises a journey of discovery and delight.

- Berat: City of a Thousand Windows

Nestled among the breathtaking landscapes of Albania, Berat emerges as a captivating city that whispers tales of history, culture, and architectural marvels. Often referred to as the "City of a Thousand Windows," Berat beckons travelers with its enchanting Ottoman-era houses, ancient citadel, and the tranquil Osum River that meanders through its heart.

1. Departure from Tirana:
Commence your journey from Tirana, embarking on a scenic drive that unveils the beauty of Albania's countryside. The anticipation grows as you draw closer to Berat, a city that promises an immersion into its rich tapestry of heritage.

2. Berat Castle:
The towering Berat Castle dominates the skyline and beckons you to explore its historical corridors. Dating back to the 4th century BC, this fortress offers

panoramic vistas of the city and the surrounding landscapes. As you meander through its labyrinthine paths, discover the secrets and stories etched into its ancient walls.

3. Mangalem Quarter:
Step into the Mangalem Quarter, where the essence of Berat's charm truly comes alive. Ottoman-style houses adorned with intricate wooden windows create a picturesque tableau that captures the imagination. Stroll along the cobblestone streets, marveling at the architectural symphony that defines this iconic neighborhood.

4. Onufri Museum:
Immerse yourself in the world of art at the Onufri Museum, nestled within the Dormition Cathedral. Named after the renowned Albanian iconographer Onufri, this museum houses a treasure trove of religious icons, frescoes, and manuscripts that offer a glimpse into the spiritual and artistic legacy of the region.

5. Ethnographic Museum:
Step inside an 18th-century Ottoman house, now the home of Berat's Ethnographic Museum. This immersive experience delves into the everyday life and traditions of Berat's inhabitants, with exhibits showcasing traditional attire, crafts, and domestic artifacts.

6. Gorica Bridge and Quarter:
Cross the historic Gorica Bridge, an architectural gem that spans the tranquil Osum River. On the opposite side, the Gorica Quarter beckons with its well-preserved homes and serene ambiance. Wander along the riverbank, where the soothing sounds of water accompany your exploration.

7. Savory Delights:
Indulge in the flavors of Berat with a delectable Albanian meal at a local restaurant. Savor traditional dishes such as petulla, tave kosi, and other regional specialties as you soak in the distinctive atmosphere of the city.

8. Helveti Teqe and Sufi Lodges:
Explore the Helveti Teqe, a historic Sufi lodge that offers a glimpse into the spiritual practices of the Bektashi order. The tranquil setting and intricate architecture create an atmosphere of introspection and serenity.

9. Sunset Serenity:
Return to Berat Castle in the evening and witness the city transform as the sun begins its descent. The warm hues of twilight cast a magical glow upon the ancient houses, providing a serene backdrop for reflection and appreciation.

Berat beckons you to partake in its history, to wander through its storied streets, and to be swept away by its architectural beauty. As the "City of a Thousand Windows," Berat invites you to step into a realm where every window holds a story, and every corner is a testament to the enduring spirit of Albania's cultural heritage.

- Shkodra: Where History and Nature Converge

Let's talk about Shkodra – a pretty cool place where history and nature come together in a seriously awesome way. Imagine walking through streets that have seen centuries of stories, all while being surrounded by the beauty of nature. It's like stepping into a time machine that takes you to a whole different world.

1. Getting Started:
So, you're all set to check out Shkodra? Awesome! Get ready for a journey that's not just about going somewhere, but about discovering a whole bunch of stories from the past and soaking up the amazing natural vibes.

2. The Castle Chronicles:
Alright, first stop – Rozafa Castle. This place is like a living history book. You can practically feel the stories seeping out of the walls as you explore. Imagine what it was like to live here back in the day – it's like connecting with history on a whole new level.

3. Picture Perfect:

Now, here's something cool – the Marubi National Museum of Photography. It's like flipping through a photo album of Shkodra's past. Those old photographs give you a glimpse of what life was like way back when. It's like stepping into a time capsule.

4. Chillin' by the Lake:
Oh, Lake Shkodra, you're like a real-life painting. The water's so calm, and it's surrounded by these beautiful wetlands and mountains. It's like a little slice of paradise where you can just take a breather and soak in all that natural goodness.

5. Village Vibes:
Now, you've got to check out Shiroka village. It's like going back in time. The simplicity of life here is refreshing, and you'll feel like you've stepped into a whole different world where time moves a bit slower.

6. Strolling in the Venetian Quarter:
Okay, so the Venetian Quarter is a total blast from the past. The buildings here have these intricate details that tell stories of times gone by. Walking through these streets is like being part of a history lesson, but a super fun one.

7. Crossing Bridges and Rivers:
Crossing the Grunasi Bridge over the Buna River is kind of magical. It's like a moment of zen, where you can just chill and watch the water flow. It's a good reminder that nature's beauty is sometimes the best way to unwind.

8. Groovin' to Shkodra's Beat:
The music scene in Shkodra is totally rad. It's like the city's heartbeats are turned into melodies. You'll find yourself tapping your foot to the rhythm and feeling like you're part of something bigger.

9. A Melting Pot of Beliefs:
Shkodra's got this unique blend of beliefs and traditions. From pagan festivals to Christian shrines, it's like the city's saying, "Hey, we're all different, but we're all part of the same story."

10. Taking Shkodra with You:
When it's time to say goodbye to Shkodra, know that the memories you've made aren't going anywhere. They'll be with you, a reminder that you've been part of something pretty special. So, keep those stories close as you keep on exploring the world.

- Theth: Alpine Adventure

Hey there, adventure seeker! If you're up for some seriously breathtaking alpine vibes, Theth is the place to be. Picture rugged mountains, lush valleys, and a vibe that's all about reconnecting with nature in its purest form.

1. Getting Ready for Theth:

Alright, gear up for an adventure that's going to take you to the heart of the Albanian Alps. Theth is like a hidden gem nestled in these majestic mountains. It's not just a place, it's an experience.

2. The Majestic Grunas Waterfall:
First stop, the Grunas Waterfall. Imagine standing in front of this towering cascade of water, feeling the cool mist on your face. It's like nature's own spa treatment. And the best part? The journey to get there is like a mini-hike through some seriously epic landscapes.

3. The Thethi National Park:
Oh, the Thethi National Park is like a playground for nature lovers. You've got hiking trails that wind through valleys, rivers, and forests. It's like stepping into a real-life painting where every step is a new adventure.

4. Lock-in at the Lock-in Tower:
You've got to check out the Lock-in Tower, a seriously ancient structure that's seen its fair share of history. Just imagine standing where people from centuries ago stood, looking out at the same epic views. It's like time traveling without the DeLorean.

5. Blue Eye: Nature's Masterpiece:
No, it's not a superhero's secret hideout – it's the Blue Eye spring. Seriously, this place is like a natural wonder. The crystal-clear blue water will make you feel like you're in another world. It's like nature's little surprise in the middle of the mountains.

6. Traditional Thethi Architecture:
Take a stroll through the village, and you'll be treated to some seriously charming traditional architecture. The stone roofs, the cozy houses – it's like stepping into a storybook village. And the locals? They're as warm as the fireplace in a log cabin.

7. Breathtaking Peaks:
If you're into hiking, you're in for a treat. Theth is surrounded by peaks that are just begging to be conquered. So, lace up those hiking boots, grab your backpack, and get ready for some seriously epic summit views.

8. River Adventure:
The Theth River is like your very own adventure playground. You can go for a refreshing dip, try your hand at fishing, or just chill by the riverside and let the sound of the flowing water wash your worries away.

9. Cultural Immersion:
Oh, and don't miss out on getting to know the local culture. The people here are super friendly and proud of their heritage. So, chat with the locals, try some traditional dishes, and soak up the genuine Albanian hospitality.

Theth is like a playground for nature enthusiasts, a place where every corner is an opportunity for adventure. It's not just a destination; it's a chance to disconnect from the hustle and bustle and reconnect with the awe-inspiring beauty of the great outdoors. So, pack your bags and get ready for an alpine adventure that you won't forget.

Chapter 8

Practical Information

- Getting to Tirana

The journey to Tirana, the capital city of Albania, is an exciting odyssey that brings you into the heart of this dynamic Balkan nation. Whether you're arriving by air, land, or sea, the path to Tirana is a prelude to the enchanting experiences that await you.If you're taking to the skies, your adventure begins as the plane touches down at Tirana International Airport Nënë Tereza. As you step onto the tarmac, the warmth of the Albanian sun greets you, setting the tone for your journey ahead. The airport buzzes with a blend of languages and cultures, a testament to Tirana's role as a hub of exploration.

From the airport, the journey into the city unveils Albania's picturesque landscapes. Mountains, valleys, and quaint villages dance by, offering glimpses of the country's rich natural beauty. The road to Tirana winds through these scenic vistas, gradually transitioning from rural serenity to the vibrant urban rhythm.For the adventurers who prefer the road, highways converge upon Tirana from various directions. Each kilometer traveled is a step deeper into Albania's allure. Quaint towns and roadside cafés dot the journey, tempting you to pause and savor the local flavors.If your voyage takes you by rail, the rhythmic clatter of the tracks becomes a musical backdrop to your anticipation. Train windows frame shifting landscapes, narrating tales of changing terrain and rural life. And as the train arrives at the station, you're greeted by the vibrant pulse of Tirana.Approaching Tirana by any means is an immersion into the city's vibrant energy. The streets bustle with life – a symphony of honking horns, animated conversations, and the scents of street food. Every corner reveals a new facet of Tirana's identity, from its historical landmarks to its modern urban districts.

As the cityscape comes into focus, landmarks like Skanderbeg Square and the iconic Pyramid make their grand entrance. Streets lined with shops, cafés, and colorful architecture beckon you to explore further. With every step, you become a part of Tirana's story, a chapter in its ongoing narrative.Getting to Tirana is more than just transportation; it's an introduction to Albania's warmth, its history, and its future. It's a gateway to the heart of a nation that embraces tradition while embracing change. So, as you embark on this journey, remember that getting to Tirana is just the beginning of the adventure that awaits you.

About Tirana International Airport
Tirana International Airport (TIA) rests just 18km away from the heart of the city. Despite being the country's

main gateway, it retains a cozy atmosphere. The early hours often see a flurry of arrivals, making it essential to plan your journey from Tirana airport to the city center in advance for seamless transportation.

Upon landing, the airport extends the convenience of free WiFi. Beyond the arrivals gate, a cluster of eager faces awaits the travelers. Separating the arrivals hall from the check-in area are a few shops and cafes. A right turn leads to the check-in zone, accompanied by the presence of ATM machines. A leftward stroll, on the other hand, guides you beyond the airport's confines.

Venturing into the departures area reveals duty-free treasures, awaiting only those who've navigated passport control.

Tirana Airport's infrastructure defies its modest size. Departing passengers can even undergo a PCR test on-site—an aspect we'll delve into. Outside, money exchange bureaux and car rental counters are within reach. And when considering the journey from Tirana airport to the city center, the options unfurl.

Tirana Airport Transfer
Foresight led me to secure my Tirana Airport transfer ahead of time. My choice was Kiwi Taxi, a steadfast companion across various global airports. Booking the transfer on the day of travel bore swift fruit, as an hour later, the driver reached out via WhatsApp. The details solidified, the drive promised familiarity in a foreign land.

An economy car conveyed me for 24 euros, with the option for more opulent vehicles.

Tirana Airport Taxi
Opting for a Tirana Airport taxi reveals a pleasant surprise: unlicensed drivers do not loiter as they might elsewhere. Legitimate options stand by the arrivals terminal, their fixed charge at 2500 leke, about 20 euros.

Tirana Airport Bus
Should frugality beckon, consider the Tirana Airport bus. An hourly service commences at 8 am and concludes at midnight, a budget-friendly choice, albeit location-dependent. Its minibus form offers comfort and speed, departing from outside the airport. The 300 leke fare can be paid in either leke or euros, the latter costing 3 euros for the sake of convenience.

For the return, make your way to the small park behind Skanderbeg Square. The shuttle bus departs every hour from 7 am to 11 pm, a reliable connection back to Tirana Airport.

- Getting Around the City

Using the Bus
The primary mode of public transportation in Tirana is the bus system, offering affordable trips at around 40 LEK. Look for buses labeled "Unaza," which follow

circular routes around the city center. While there isn't a central bus station, you'll find various bus stops conveniently scattered throughout the city.

Opting for Furgons
Furgons, or minibuses, represent a privately-owned public transportation option. These larger vans display their chosen destinations in their front windows. Simply wave down a furgon, and if there's space, they'll stop to pick you up.

Embracing Bicycles
Tirana is increasingly bicycle-friendly, with dedicated lanes sprouting across the city. The Ecovolis Bicycle Sharing Program, launched in 2011, provides rental stations including Rinia Park and Deshmoret e Kombit Boulevard. For a full day's use, pay 100 LEK, and remember to return the bicycle to its original station. Rruga Qemal Stafa is a hub for bike rentals, and designated bicycle lanes can be found along Skanderbeg Square, Deshmoret e Kombit Main Boulevard, Lana River sidewalks, and Kavaja Street.

Strolling on Foot
Embarking on foot is a fantastic way to uncover Tirana's charm, especially since the city center is compact enough for leisurely exploration. A single day allows you to traverse the central area, visiting museums, monuments, historical sites, and parks. Enjoy the main streets at your own pace, pausing for coffee breaks, snacks, and shopping. Day or night, walking through

Tirana, you'll find rewards in every corner. Guided walking tours are also available, ensuring you experience must-see spots like BunkArt and Blloku, while savoring Albanian street food along the way.

Driving the Streets
Renting a car might not be necessary when exploring Tirana unless you're venturing outside the city or planning countrywide exploration. With public transport available within the city and most attractions a short walk from the downtown area, you'll find convenience without a car. Keep in mind that parking can be scarce and costly. Also, remember that some roads in Albania may not be in pristine condition, and adherence to traffic lights can be inconsistent.

Hailing Taxis
Taxis are abundant throughout Tirana, offering a convenient mode of transportation. Whether by the city center, major attractions, hotels, or restaurants, you'll find taxis ready for service. You can also book one via phone through your hotel. It's wise to agree on a fare before starting your ride, and some drivers might even offer affordable area tours.

- Accommodation Options

When it comes to accommodation options in Tirana, you'll find a diverse range to suit every traveler's needs and preferences. From luxury hotels to cozy guesthouses, the city offers a variety of places to stay that cater to different budgets and tastes.

Luxury Hotels
For those seeking a lavish stay, Tirana boasts a selection of high-end luxury hotels that provide top-notch amenities and services. Enjoy elegantly designed rooms, spa facilities, fine dining restaurants, and stunning city views. Whether you're here for business or leisure, these hotels offer a lavish retreat in the heart of the city.

Boutique Hotels
Boutique hotels in Tirana offer a unique and personalized experience. These smaller, independently-owned properties often focus on providing intimate and stylish accommodations. You can expect thoughtfully designed rooms, personalized service, and a cozy atmosphere that sets them apart from larger chain hotels.

Mid-Range Hotels
Mid-range hotels offer a comfortable stay without breaking the bank. These hotels provide modern amenities, well-appointed rooms, and often include on-site dining options. They strike a balance between affordability and quality, making them a popular choice for many travelers.

Guesthouses and Bed & Breakfasts
For a more local and intimate experience, consider staying at a guesthouse or bed & breakfast. These accommodations often offer a warm and welcoming environment, allowing you to interact with locals and fellow travelers. Enjoy home-cooked breakfasts and a cozy ambiance that makes you feel right at home.

Hostels
Tirana also offers several hostels catering to budget-conscious travelers and backpackers. Hostels provide shared dormitory-style rooms, which are an excellent way to meet fellow travelers from around the world. Many hostels offer communal spaces, kitchen facilities, and social activities that encourage interaction among guests.

Apartment Rentals
If you prefer more space and the convenience of a home-like environment, consider renting an apartment or a serviced apartment. This option is ideal for families or travelers who want the flexibility of cooking their meals and having a living space to relax in.

Choosing Your Accommodation
When selecting your accommodation in Tirana, consider factors such as location, budget, and the amenities that matter most to you. Whether you're looking for a luxurious escape, a cozy retreat, or a budget-friendly stay, Tirana offers a wide range of accommodation options to make your stay comfortable and enjoyable. Remember to book in advance, especially during peak travel seasons, to secure the best options for your trip.

Here are some of my best hotels in Tirana

Note:Please make an effort to conduct further research in order to find the accommodation option that best suits your needs.
1. Rogner Hotel Tirana
2. Maritim Hotel Plaza Tirana
3. Hilton Garden Inn Tirana
4. Hotel Mondial
5. Xheko Imperial Hotel & SPA
6. Dinasty Hotel
7. Mak Albania Hotel
8. Hotel Opera
9. La Boheme Hotel
10. Tirana International Hotel & Conference Centre
11. Hotel Elisa Tirana, Affiliated By Meliá
12. Sar'Otel Boutique Hotel
13. Tirana Marriott Hotel
14. Bujtina e Gjelit
15. Metro Hotel Tirana

16. Hotel Baron
17. Hotel Boutique Kotoni
18. Hotel Colosseo Tirana
19. Hotel Boutique Gloria
20. Theranda Hotel

Cheap Hotels in Tirana

Comfy stays at affordable prices, with plenty of options in popular neighborhoods.

1. Hotel Opera
2. Hotel Baron
3. City Hotel Tirana
4. Jolly Hotel
5. Bujtina e Gjelit
6. Hotel Millennium
7. Areela Boutique Hotel
8. VH Broadway Tirana Hotel
9. Hotel Nobel
10. Hotel Boutique Vila Verde

- Safety Tips and Emergency Contacts

Tirana is generally a safe city for travelers, but like any destination, it's important to take precautions to ensure your safety during your stay. Here are some safety tips to keep in mind:

1. Stay Aware: Be aware of your surroundings, especially in crowded areas and tourist spots. Keep an eye on your belongings and avoid displaying expensive items.

2. Use Reliable Transportation: Opt for official taxis or ride-sharing services, and avoid accepting rides from unlicensed drivers. If you're using public transportation, be cautious of your belongings.

3. Secure Accommodation: Choose reputable accommodations and lock your room or apartment when you're not inside. Use hotel safes to store valuables.

4. Stay Hydrated and Sun-Safe: Tirana can have hot summers, so drink plenty of water and wear sunscreen to protect yourself from the sun.

5. Respect Local Customs: Familiarize yourself with local customs and etiquette to avoid unintentionally offending locals.

6. Avoid Petty Crimes: Petty crimes like pickpocketing can occur in crowded areas. Keep your belongings secure, use money belts or hidden pouches, and avoid carrying large amounts of cash.

7. Emergency Contacts:*

  - **Police:** 129
  - **Ambulance:** 127
  - **Fire Department:** 128

8. Healthcare: Familiarize yourself with the location of medical facilities in the area you're staying. If you need medical assistance, contact your embassy or consulate for guidance.

9. Travel Insurance: Before your trip, make sure you have comprehensive travel insurance that covers medical emergencies, trip cancellations, and other unexpected events.

10. Local Laws: Obey local laws and regulations to avoid legal troubles. Familiarize yourself with the local laws and customs before your trip.

11. Emergency Numbers: Keep a list of emergency numbers, including your country's embassy or consulate, in case you need assistance.

Remember that staying safe is a shared responsibility. By staying vigilant and following these safety tips, you can have a worry-free and enjoyable experience in Tirana.

- Useful Phrases for Travelers

While many locals in Tirana may speak English, making an effort to use a few basic Albanian phrases can enhance your travel experience and show your appreciation for the local culture. Here are some useful phrases to keep in mind:

1. **Hello: Tungjatjeta (TOON-jah-tye-tah)**

2. **Goodbye:** Mirupafshim (mee-roo-PAHF-shim)
3. **Please:** Të lutem (tuh LOO-tehm)
4. **Thank you:** Faleminderit (FAH-leh-meen-deh-reet)
5. **Yes:** Po (poh)
6. **No:** Jo (yoh)
7. **Excuse me / Sorry:** Më fal (muh fahl)
8. **I don't understand:** Nuk kuptoj (nook KOOPT-oy)
9. **How much is this?:** Sa kushton kjo? (sah KOOHS-tohn k-yoh?)
10. **Where is...?:** Ku është...? (koo uhs-TUH...?)
11. **Bathroom:** Banjo (BAHN-yoh)
12. **Help:** Ndihmë (ndee-HM)
13. **I'm lost:** Jam humbur (yahm hoom-BOOR)
14. **Can you help me?:** Mund të më ndihmoni? (moond tuh muh ndee-HMOH-nee?)
15. **Water:** Ujë (OO-yuh)
16. **Food:** Ushqim (oosh-KEEM)
17. **I need a doctor:** Më duhet një doktor (muh DOO-heht nyuh DOHK-tohr)
18. **I'm allergic to...:** Jam alergjik ndaj... (yahm ah-LEHR-jik n-dai...)
19. **I'm vegetarian:** Jam bariatar (yahm bahr-yah-TAHR)
20. **Cheers!:** Gëzuar! (guh-ZOO-ahr)
21. **My name is...:** Emri im është... (EHM-ree ihm uhs-TUH...)
22. **What's your name?:** Si quheni? (see KOO-heh-nee?)

Using these phrases can help you navigate through everyday situations and connect with locals in Tirana. The effort you make to communicate in their language is sure to be appreciated and may even lead to some memorable interactions during your trip.

- Conversion Charts and Measurements

Currency's exchange
* The official currency in Albania is the lek (ALL).
* Euros are also widely accepted in Tirana, so you can exchange your currency for euros before you travel, or you can exchange your currency for lek at the airport or at any bank in Tirana.
* The exchange rate for the lek fluctuates, so it is always a good idea to check the latest exchange rate before you exchange your currency.
* You can exchange your currency at the airport, at banks, or at currency exchange bureaus. The exchange rate may be better at currency exchange bureaus, but they may charge a commission.
* It is a good idea to keep some lek in small denominations for small purchases.

Here are some places where you can exchange currency in Tirana:

* The airport
* Banks
* Currency exchange bureaus

* Hotels
* Some shops and restaurants

Here are some tips for exchanging currency in Tirana:

* Compare the exchange rates before you exchange your currency.
* Be aware of the fees that may be charged.
* Only exchange the amount of currency that you need.
* Keep your exchange receipt in case you need to exchange your currency back.

-Dress Comfortably and Stylishly in Vibrant Tirana!

As you prepare to explore the charming streets of Tirana, Albania, you'll want to strike the perfect balance between comfort and style. The city's lively atmosphere, diverse culture, and pleasant climate call for an outfit that adapts seamlessly to various activities and occasions. Here's your guide to dressing smartly and confidently while experiencing the best of Tirana:

Daytime Adventures:

- **Casual Attire**: Opt for light, breathable fabrics like cotton and linen to combat Tirana's warm daytime temperatures.

- **Comfortable Shoes**: Walking is the best way to explore, so choose comfortable sneakers or walking shoes.
- **Sunglasses & Hat:** Shield yourself from the sun with a pair of stylish sunglasses and a wide-brimmed hat.

- **Modesty in Mind:** While Tirana is open-minded, it's respectful to cover your shoulders and knees when visiting religious sites.

Evening Delights:

- **Casual Elegance:** Tirana's nightlife calls for chic yet relaxed outfits. Think stylish dresses, button-up shirts, or well-fitted jeans.

- **Layers:** Evenings can be cooler, so consider carrying a light jacket or cardigan.

- **Versatile Footwear:** Choose comfortable shoes that match your outfit and are suitable for both strolling and dancing.

Dining Out:

- **Smart-Casual**: Many restaurants embrace a smart-casual dress code. Dress up a bit, but feel free to infuse your personal style.

- **Footwear:** Opt for closed-toe shoes or sandals that are appropriate for a nicer setting.

Capture Memories:

- **Camera-Friendly**: Tirana's colorful streets and vibrant markets are perfect for photos. Dress comfortably yet stylishly to ensure you're ready for impromptu snapshots.

Shopping Spree:

- **Comfortable Shoes:** A good pair of walking shoes will make exploring Tirana's boutiques and bazaars a breeze.

- **Easy-to-Remove Layers:** Since you'll be trying on clothes, consider an outfit that's easy to change in and out of.

Cultural Visits:

- **Respectful Attire:** If you're visiting cultural or religious sites, choose outfits that cover your shoulders, knees, and midriff.

- **Shawl or Scarf:** Carrying a shawl or scarf in your bag will help you adapt to any dress code requirements.

Packing Essentials:

-**Sunscreen**:Protect your skin from Tirana's sunny days.

- **Reusable Water Bottle:** Stay hydrated while you explore.

- **Umbrella:** Just in case of sudden rain showers.

- **Adaptable Outfits**: Consider mix-and-match pieces that offer versatility for various activities.

Remember, the key is to feel comfortable, confident, and ready to embrace Tirana's unique energy. Pack an outfit for every occasion, while keeping in mind the weather and cultural considerations. With the right attire, you'll be ready to create wonderful memories in this vibrant city!

Conclusion

In conclusion, the Tirana Travel Guide 2023/2024 is your ultimate companion for unlocking the heart and soul of this vibrant city. As you've journeyed through the pages of this guide, you've discovered not only the historical and cultural treasures that Tirana offers but also the immersive experiences that allow you to truly connect with the city like a local.From savoring the delectable flavors of traditional Albanian cuisine to exploring the captivating landmarks that tell the story of Tirana's past and present, this guide has provided you with insights and tips to make the most of your visit. You've learned about the hidden gems that lie beyond the tourist's gaze, the serene river embankments perfect for strolls, the bustling bazaars brimming with local crafts, and the lively nightlife that keeps the city alive after the sun sets.

But this journey is just the beginning. Armed with the knowledge of where to go, what to eat, how to navigate, and how to connect with the locals, you're poised to embark on an unforgettable adventure through the colorful streets of Tirana.The Tirana Travel Guide 2023 isn't just a book – it's a ticket to a personalized experience, a gateway to new friendships, and a roadmap to creating lasting memories. So pack your bags, follow your curiosity, and let the city of Tirana unfold before your eyes. Whether you're a first-time traveler or a returning visitor, this guide ensures that every step you take is guided by authenticity, curiosity, and a deep appreciation for the beauty that Tirana holds.As you step into the vibrant tapestry of Tirana, remember that the stories you'll uncover, the flavors you'll savor, and the connections you'll forge will all be uniquely yours. Let the Tirana Travel Guide 2023 be your trusty companion, inspiring you to explore, connect, and experience the city in ways you never imagined.The journey is yours – make it extraordinary with the Tirana Travel Guide 2023. Start your adventure today and see the city through new eyes.

Thank you for choosing the Tirana Travel Guide 2023 to enhance your journey through the captivating city of Tirana. We sincerely hope this guide has enriched your experience and allowed you to delve deeper into the city's culture, history, and hidden gems. Your feedback is invaluable to us, and we would greatly appreciate it if you could take a moment to share your thoughts by leaving a review on Amazon. Your insights will not only help us improve but also guide fellow travelers in making the most of their Tirana adventure. Safe travels and happy exploring!

Bonus Chapter

Tirana Travel Journal

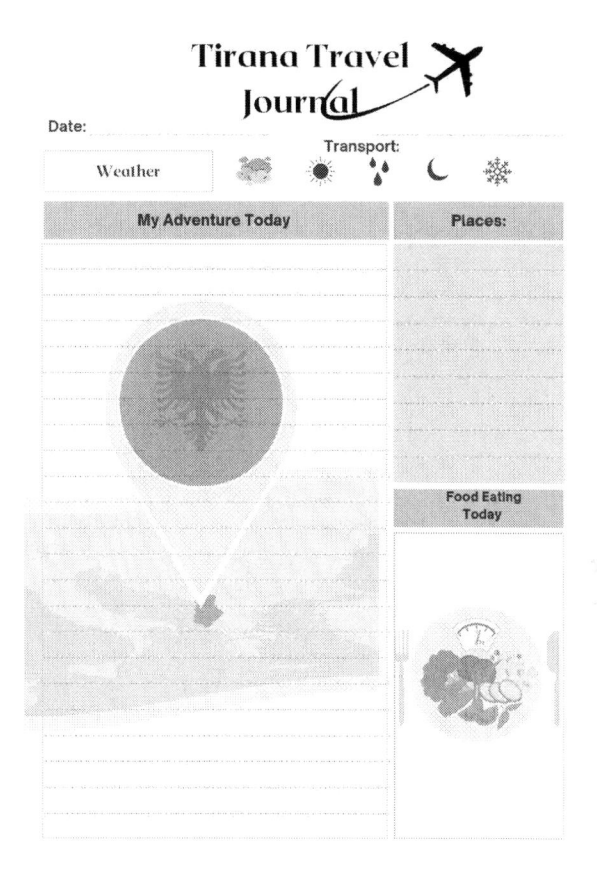

Tirana Travel Journal

Date: _____

Transport:

Weather

My Adventure Today

Places:

Food Eating Today

Tirana Travel Journal

Date:

Transport:

Weather

My Adventure Today

Places:

Food Eating Today

Tirana Travel Journal

Date:

Transport:

Weather

My Adventure Today

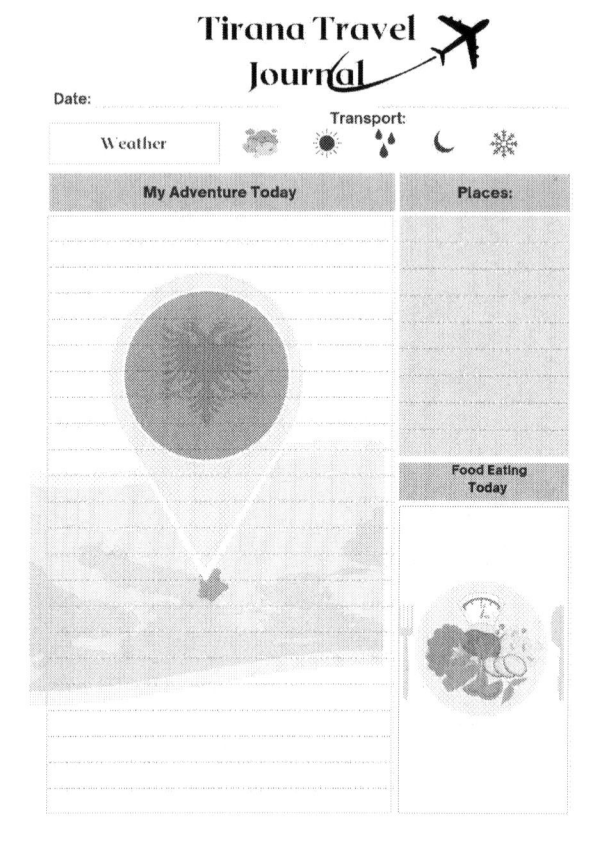

Places:

Food Eating Today

Tirana Travel Journal

Date:

Transport:

Weather

My Adventure Today

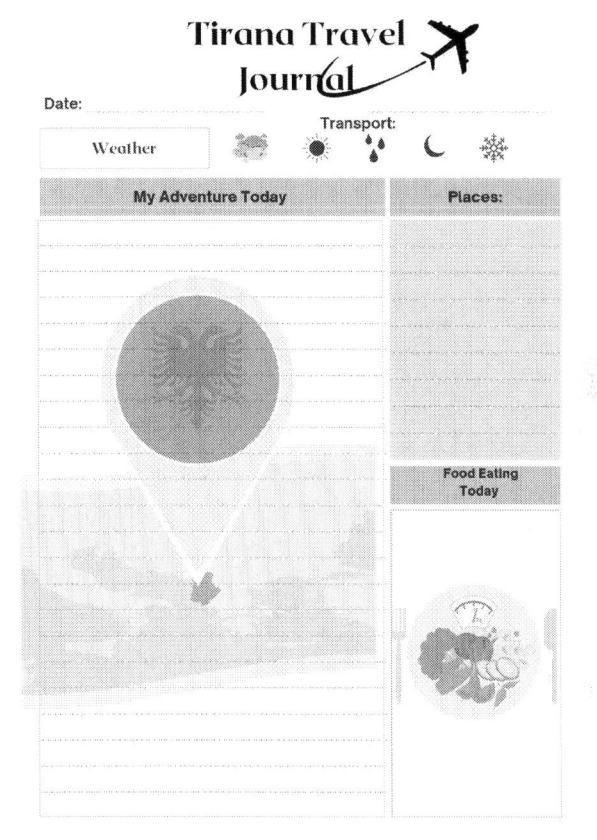

Places:

Food Eating Today

Tirana Travel Journal

Date:

Transport:

Weather

My Adventure Today

Places:

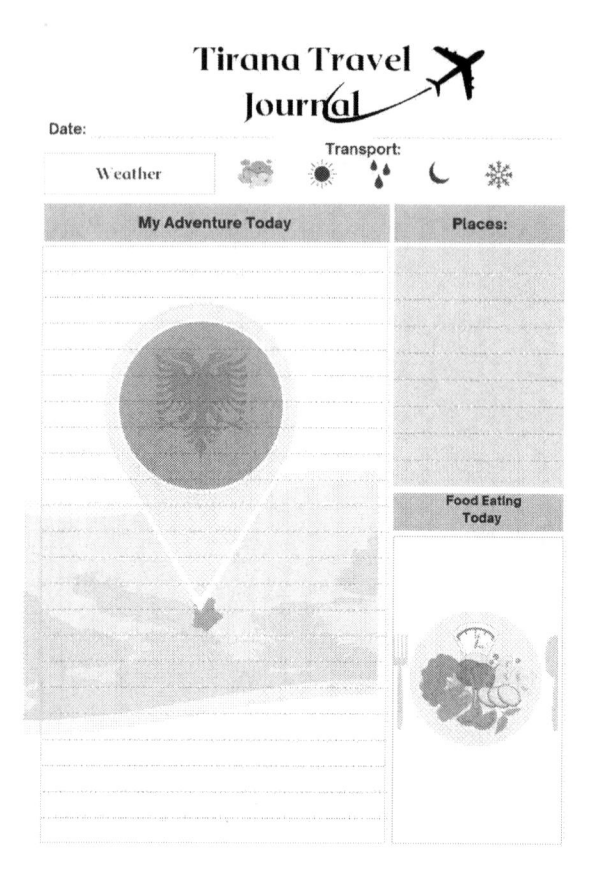

Food Eating Today

143

Tirana Travel Journal

Date:

Transport:

Weather

My Adventure Today

Places:

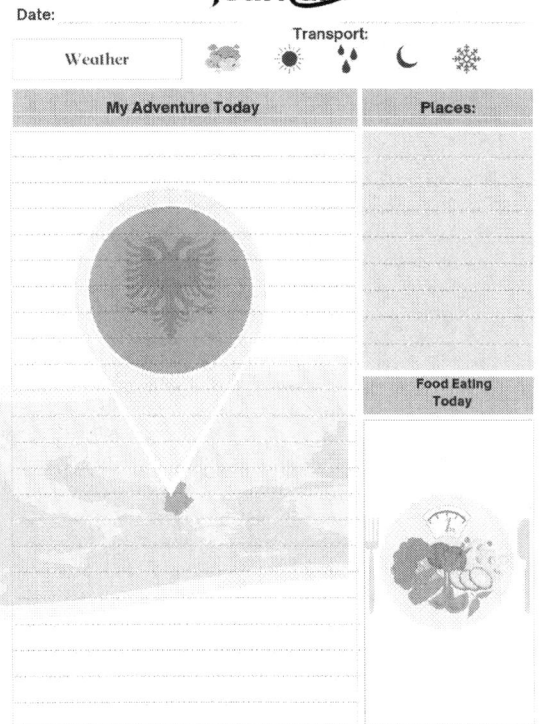

Food Eating Today

Tirana Travel Journal

Date:

Weather

Transport:

My Adventure Today

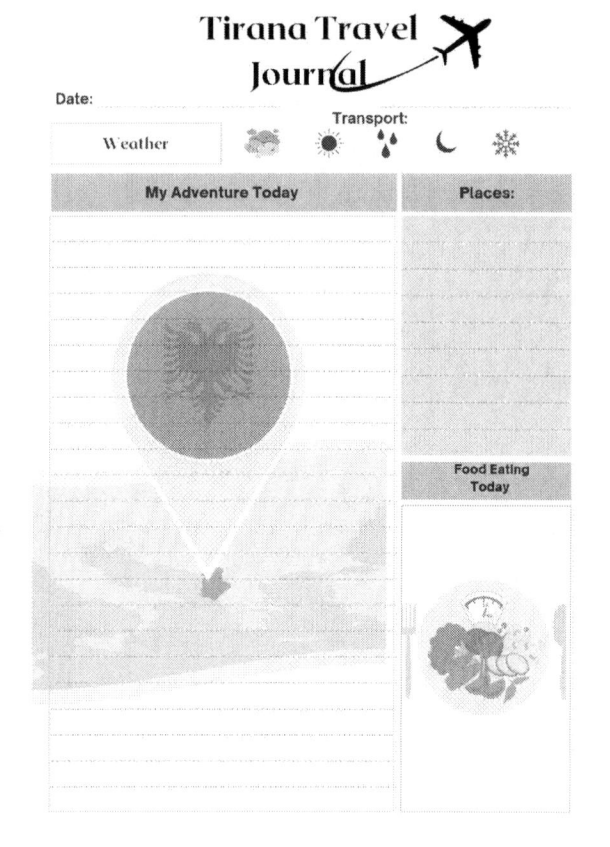

Places:

Food Eating Today

Tirana Travel Journal

Date: _____

Transport:

Weather

My Adventure Today

Places:

Food Eating Today

Tirana Travel Journal

Date:

Weather   **Transport:**

My Adventure Today

Places:

Food Eating Today

Tirana Travel Journal

Date: _____

Transport: _____

Weather: _____

My Adventure Today

Places:

Food Eating Today

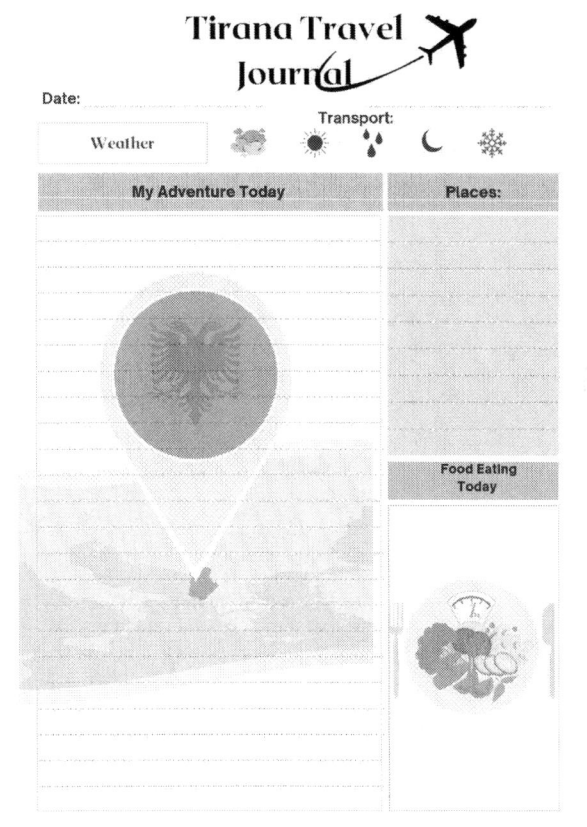

Tirana Travel Journal

Date:

Transport:

Weather

My Adventure Today

Places:

Food Eating Today

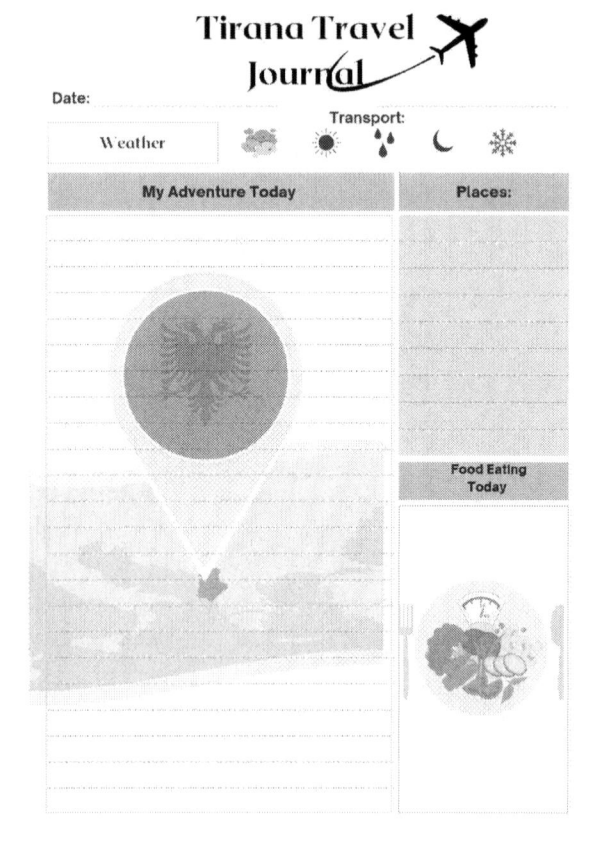

Tirana Travel Journal ✈

Date: _____

Transport:

| Weather | ☁ ☀ 💧 ☾ ❄ |

My Adventure Today

Places:

Food Eating Today

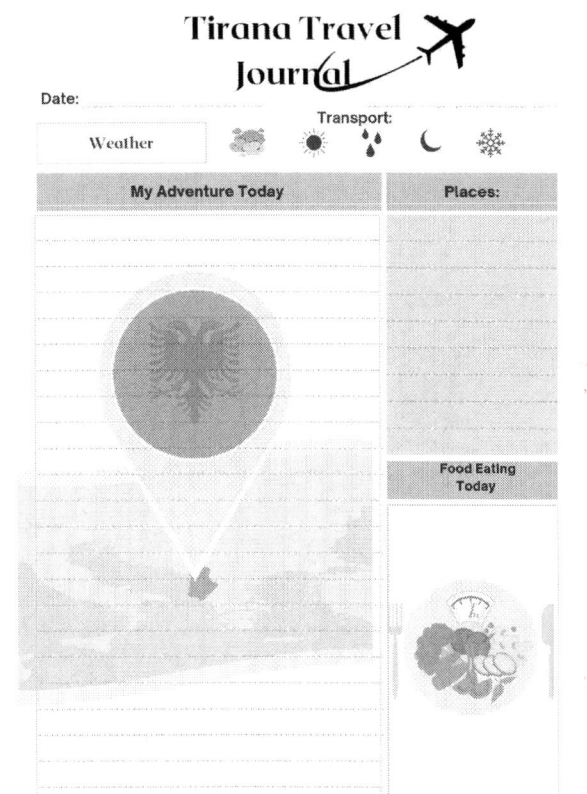

Tirana Travel Journal

Date:

Transport:

Weather

My Adventure Today

Places:

Food Eating Today

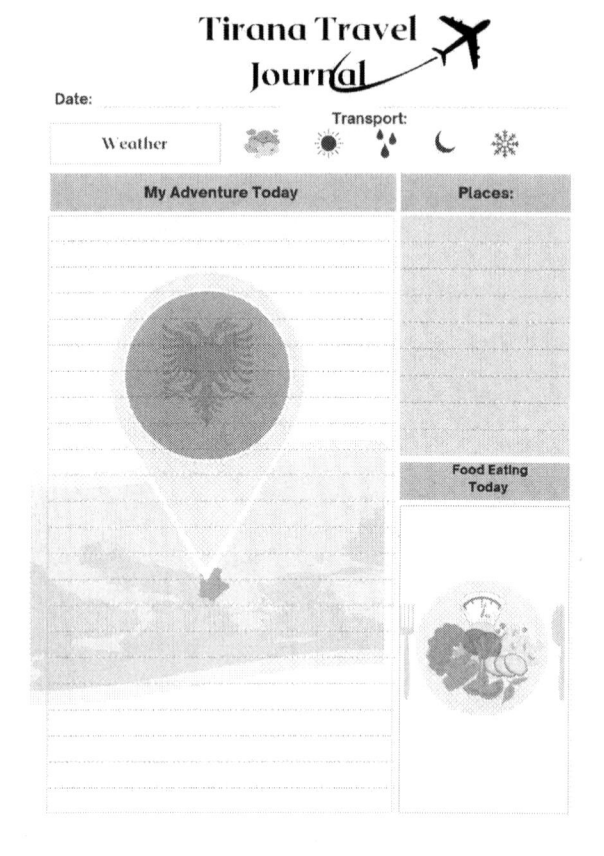

Printed in Great Britain
by Amazon